MW00614068

The Meditation Book

The Essential Meditation for Beginners to Find Peace, Reduce Stress, and Improve Mental Health

Blair Abee

Energetic Wave Publishing
Vallejo, California

Blair Abee/Energetic Wave Publishing
139 Dyer Ct.
Vallejo, Ca. 94591
www.HiCMeditation.com

Book Layout ©2017 BookDesignTemplates.com V1.1

Ordering Information:
Quantity sales. Special discounts are available on quantity purchases by corporations, associations, and others. For details, contact the "Special Sales Department" at the address above.

The Meditation Book/ Blair Abee. —2nd ed.
ISBN 978-1-7344754-8-7

Contents

CHAPTER 1

You.......Me........We are All Eternal Beings

While this book is for beginners, experienced meditations will love it as well. This book will introduce you the two main types of meditation—sit-down meditation and mindfulness meditation techniques, both of which complement each other. I also offer new techniques that I have developed that will soon have you achieving Elevated Awareness, Higher Consciousness, which takes years to develop using traditional methods.

The practical benefits of meditation will quickly become available to you—physical, mental, emotional, and spiritual benefits. Benefits, that are discussed in detail in my first book, The Amazing Benefits of Meditation, like:

- Stress reduction
- A strengthened immune system
- Lowered chance of heart disease
- Improved emotional I.Q.

This book will also give you a better sense of yourself, in particular your Higher Self, or the Soul part of you, which many of us don't know much about. And don't have much experience of.

Let me start by offering with might sound like a radical idea. An idea which almost all religions offer as a tenant of their teachings. That when we die, pass over to the Other Side, we will retain some semblance of our consciousness, our essence, to go on to Heaven or Nirvana, to reside there forever or to get ready to come back to the earth again in a new human form—reincarnation.

While the details differ, the core concept is that we are Eternal Beings

More accurately, you and I are Eternity......Being Itself. At the leading edge of evolution. The Universe unfolding moment by moment. Think about that for a bit. More importantly, feel that. Doesn't your heart soar with that thought? That you are Eternity at this moment unfolding itself as You. Even for just an instant? Yes? That's one of the things you came here to Planet Earth to learn. To experience. To Know. To remember.

Within you, infusing you, is your Soul, your Higher Consciousness, Spirit, just waiting to be acknowledged. Communed with. Allowed to participate with the human you about to become if you can just remember Who You Are this lifetime. That's what this book is about. Remembering. Remembering your Divine Nature.

Imagine you are standing on the cliff in Heaven. You've decided which two Earthlings, also Eternal Beings, you are going to enter Earth's portal through. You know the circumstances that you will be encountering and what you will be undertaking. You are excited to be going to Earth. It's kind of like boot camp. Hot and sticky in the summertime; harsh. Fun. Bracing. Another opportunity to grow, and expand, and be with your Eternal Being Soul Group, including your challenging big brother who has bugged and loved you for many a lifetime.

And you jump. Down the chute. A bit like the water slide flume at Disneyland. Plop. Somebody catches you. You take your first breath. And the fun begins.

CHAPTER 2

Illumination

This is a different type of meditation book. (For my Christian friends, meditation and silent prayer are the same thing). The book's purpose is your **illumination**. Its goal is a **fundamental shift** in your ground of being, from three-dimensional, everyday consciousness, to Five-Dimensional, **Soul Consciousness**. The means to accomplish the purpose is a new form of meditation called **Higher Consciousness Meditation (HCM)**, which is explained in detail in Chapter 6.

Now, I know that this is a bold claim. I invite you to explore the ideas in this book, to see if they resonate and accomplish the purpose laid out above. The ideas and principals offered are not religious, but Spiritual. The meditation process, or silent prayer if you will, that I developed originally just for myself, will be helpful for followers of all religions or none at all.

I also invite you to explore the companion books to this one, The Many Benefits of Meditation: Living the Life You've Always Wanted to Live (free at my website), and Six Second

Mindfulness Meditations: Exercises to Transform any Moment (Book 3 available at Amazon Books) which explores quick "triggers" you can use throughout the day to accelerate your learning.

What is Illumination?

I think of Illumination as that feeling, that experience, of being filled with light, radiant. We can see it in a person's eyes when they glow with understanding, compassion, and love. Buddha was said to have achieved illumination or enlightenment while meditating under the Bodhi tree and brought forth teachings which have resounded throughout the centuries.

The Illumination I speak of is based on an alternative view of the world. One in which, from a higher state of awareness, the nature of reality is perceived differently. Through this illumined state of mind ordinary, everyday, three- dimensional (3d) reality, as perceived with our body/mind personality, shifts a bit and is not quite so solid and immutable. This is a shift of our perception to see the reality of another dimension, the Spirit dimension, which I call 5-Dimensional (5D) Reality.

(Note: I skip from 3d to 5D because, as Einstein correctly point out, the 4th dimension is time.)

In this shift, 3d consciousness dissolves a bit and a whole other reality, 5D Reality, comes into view. It is a mystical experience where the world of Spirit, which interpenetrates the material world, is perceived with the sacred senses of our divine nature.

The experience is one of being "lit up", vibrating at a higher frequency and filled with love, joy, peace, and other spiritual qualities. We perceive ourselves as one with the entire Universe and all its parts. Through our Soul Consciousness we perceive the realm of Spirit.

This experience of Illumination can be a momentary one or a permanent one. Most people who have this experience begin with small glimpses, which, over time, become more frequent and more sustained. Master Teachers like Buddha, Jesus, and Lao Tzu are said to have reached full Enlightenment—a state of Illumination that is continuous and sustained—and never went back to 3d consciousness. I have to say that I am a bit skeptical of the notion of "never going back". I think they must have had bad hair days from time and gotten grumpy when they hadn't had enough sleep, but I don't really know.

In any case, Jesus, and others like him are depicted as having halos around their heads. I think this is because they were so "lit up" with Spirit, radiated such love and compassion, that to the perceiver they seemed like hallowed beings. Healings happened spontaneously in their presence.

I am not promising a permanent state of Illumination with Higher Consciousness Meditation but, instead, a beginning onto the path where Enlightenment may be your experience some day. It's a journey that takes as long as it takes. Once embarked upon, however, it is **the** great adventure of the personality and the Soul together--the ultimate destination of each one of us.

My contention is that Higher Consciousness can be learned by anyone who decides to pursue it. I am offering in this book tools with which you can embark on the path and pursue personal growth and evolution. The ways and means and processes offered in this book can be used to move you in that direction, to generate great momentum and to make tremendous progress in this lifetime. A few of you may reach the stage where Enlightenment becomes your experience. Most will not, but you are setting the stage for that to occur, sometime, somewhere.

In the meantime, your quality of life is likely to improve in almost every area and you are likely to experience a sense of peace and well-being the likes of which you have never known. Your life will be more and more filled with love and joy. Those around you will perceive the difference in who you are becoming and will benefit as well. They will ask you, "What are you doing differently; have you cut your hair?" Some may drift out
of your life, unable or unwilling to stay around the more positive, enlightened you.

Benefits of this Book

The book offers a step-by-step description of Higher Consciousness Meditation, techniques, and triggers to help keep you on track, and a philosophical underpinning for the approach to
Illumination through the meditation technique offered. The potential benefits are substantial. The book can help you:

- Be more awake and aware
- Be more alive, joyful, and self-confident
- Be more peaceful and loving
- Have a stronger sense of health and well-being

- Attract good people, things, and circumstances
- Make better decisions
- Deal better with life's difficult situations

The approach is designed for beginners. The language is straightforward, and the Higher Consciousness Meditation process is simple, yet powerful. It can be done in 6 minutes or less per session. In addition, there are short forms of mindfulness meditation that can be done in as little as 6 seconds.

Experienced meditators will find this book of great interest, as well. It's easy for the experienced meditator to plateau out after having some success at stilling the mind but finding herself/himself far short of feeling awake and aware. The Higher Consciousness Meditation process, and accompanying techniques and triggers, will help the experienced meditator find a new level of enrichment in her/his practice.

This book is one of a group of books called the Higher Consciousness Series for those interested in addressing some of life's knottier problems and issues: abundance, relationships, health and healing, personal and business decision making and more.

(Please go to our website HiCMeditation.com and sign up to receive a free copy of my first book, <u>The Amazing Benefits of Meditation</u>, weekly blog posts, announcements of new books as they are published, and other items of interest. In addition, you will find articles, sample chapters, poems, and a "Healthy Home" product page to support your exploration of your path to enlightenment and well-being.

Use this information to grow and have fun. It is intended to give you tools to Wake Up. Any of them may be the key that unlocks the door to your Illumination. Your "aha" moment, when the enormity of Who You Are is experienced. And you begin to see the world with Sacred Eyes rather than just human eyes.

CHAPTER 3

My Story

A quick word about how this series of books that I am publishing is based on my study of spiritual matters over the past 46 years and the application of principals that I have learned throughout my life. In many ways, though, the impetus to write these books was born out of adversity and the need to dive deep into Spirit to deal with that adversity.

My trial by fire and my deep dive into Higher Consciousness began in earnest in early 2012 when I took a promotion and moved to San Diego to become Associate State Director of the San Diego Small Business Development Center (SBDC) Network. I had worked in the SBDC system, sponsored by the US Small Business Administration, for 19 years in North Carolina. I was particularly good at my profession and had worked my way up through the ranks with great success. San Diego was my next stop to the top of my profession--State Director.

Unfortunately, my experience in San Diego was professional hell. The San Diego Network was being managed by a poor leader and manager. She had been running the program into the ground for nearly 10 years, abusing employees, manipulating money, and confusing her lackadaisical overseers with a smoke and mirrors game of monumentally devious proportions. Program performance was abysmal. I tried to find out what was going on with the program before I accepted the job, but nobody would tell me the truth. And my wife, Lynne, and I were anxious to get back to California, after being away for 20 years. Both of our boys, their wives and our grandsons lived on the West Coast.

For more than 6 months I tried to learn my new, complex job, and use my knowledge and experience to improve the situation. I knew what needed to be done, from my previous time in North Carolina, but my ideas were rejected. I ended up in a pitch battle with my supervisor over survival of the program. She began to blame me for all the problems with the program and she threatened to have me fired as a way of diverting attention from her own incompetence.

I blew the whistle on the situation, revealing to community college officials who were supposed to be monitoring the program what was going on. And thus, ensued another 6-month period in which an investigation was done. She got demoted and eventually fired from the program. Unfortunately, I was fired too as a "troublemaker" one week before my one-year probation was up. The program is now, 4 years later, finally under competent leadership but is still at the corrupt, dysfunctional community college that is its host.

My next 12 months were exceedingly difficult, as well. For nine of them, I tried to find a suitable job in my profession. I came remarkably close to becoming a State Director several times, in the final group of two candidates twice, but with no success. The same thing happened with Associate State Director and

Center Director positions in California for which I interviewed. Each time, I came up empty handed after traveling quite a bit and interviewing a lot. I'm sure it didn't help that potential employers would contact my former employer and hear...who knows what. I also filed a whistle blower action with the California State Personnel Board but lost after a hearing in which college officials accused me of incompetence and blatantly lied about numerous facts in the case.

Throughout this whole episode, my meditation practice was one of my key anchors to maintaining a sense of well-being. It enabled me to "keep my head about me while others were losing theirs" (If by Rudyard Kipling). I was able to return over and over again to a reasonably peaceful state of mind, no matter what insanity was going on around me.

At times, my heart would soften toward those that I saw as my tormenters. I began to recognize that they were acting out of personal pain and projecting onto me the things they were not able to accept about themselves. I could see that they were doing the very best they could muster under the circumstances of their work and their lives, which had nothing to do with me. It wasn't personal.

I managed to stay "in the moment" much of the time, though there were times when I was very annoyed and upset.

I went deeper and deeper into my meditation practice and began to have amazing insights and experiences, including experiences of Illumination. And of developing a relationship with my Soul, my Higher Consciousness. I began writing about my experiences, with no thought of publishing, but as part of my healing process.

The idea that has been taught by the world's Master Teachers for centuries of Spirit being Within us, and that when we turn Within It will come flooding to meet us, began to make a lot of sense to me. In my case I think my Higher Consciousness had waited lifetimes, many lifetimes, for me to begin to Awaken and has been such a great, and patient, teacher.

This saga began to remind me of the "Hero's Journey" that Joseph Campbell speaks so eloquently of in his book Hero with A Thousand Faces. In the book he argues that many successful stories follow the same storyline development. According to Campbell, the archetypical journey begins, inevitably, with the reluctant hero launching off into a new reality (San Diego for me); having difficult, life altering adventures; discovering treasure in a far-off land; and bringing the physical treasure, or important information, back to ordinary reality to share with the village s/he left.

In my case, I have done a very deep dive into my inner Self and have discovered the gold of my Higher Consciousness. I have returned to share what I have learned with the village, so we can all celebrate in our good fortune at what I have discovered. I now see the bigger picture of the whys and wherefores of my Journey and have found that I am exactly where I was led to be, where I subconsciously wanted to be, and that I created a scenario that allow me to let go of my previous life.

Now, right this moment, I am doing exactly what I should be doing, sitting here writing this saga. My tormenters were my liberators. They forced me to step into a world of the unknown that I only had an inkling existed--a life that is enlivening, and fun, creative, and ever expanding. I am beyond forgiveness at this point and over into "Thank you, thank you, thank you" for my new life.

Questions to Consider.

At the end of each chapter I have posed experience provoking questions for your consideration. I say "experience provoking" rather than "thought provoking" because these questions, like my words already offered, are intended to take you Inside where all of your answers lie. Where your illumination resides. Take a moment and jot a note or two after each question that grabs you for your future use (if you are reading a physical book. If not start a paper or electronic meditation journal to record your experiences. A journaling app for your phone should be available in the next few months for this purpose, as well.)

Questions to Consider

Can you identify with my struggles? If so, how?

If the answer to the first question is yes, what "gold" did my story yield for you?

CHAPTER 4

Who Are We? Why Are We Here? Where Are We Going?

These are questions that mankind has asked for centuries. They are also questions that have been asked and answered by many who have endeavored to plumb the depths of the mystery that is humankind. They continue to be good questions to ask and attempt to answer. Here is my stab at it. (Keep in mind that these are my opinions and aren't meant to be a challenge to your personal beliefs.)

We were born on a relatively insignificant planet which revolves around a modest sun at the outer edge of a rather ordinary galaxy--one of many billions of such galaxies in a bewilderingly complex universe. Earth is a hard planet on which to be born. It is a tough place that requires we develop elaborate, convoluted strategies to keep ourselves clothed, fed, and housed. Our home is a place where it seems that the philosophy of "dog eat dog", survival of the fittest, predominates, causing its inhabitants to compete fiercely for limited resources.

We arrive here, Souls from the Other Side, with lofty expectations, and find that we've been born into a place where the planetary culture, including what people seem to know and accept about the place is limited, confining and smothering. Coming in we know this to be true because we've been here before, many times. (Reincarnation is a key concept in many religions. It was part of early Christian teachings until it was squashed by the Council of Nicaea in 325 AD. In fact, it was a belief that Jesus and his followers took pretty much for granted. Jesus himself speaks of John the Baptist as the return of Elias (Matthew 11:14 and 17:11, Mark 9:11-13)).

However, we forget what we know as we begin to occupy our helpless infant bodies and look to those around us for clues about how to survive. Unfortunately, almost nobody is "awake and aware", so there are few role models for that alternative; almost no one has a different view from the accepted conventional wisdom. This conventional wisdom is nearly absolute--everybody thinks, and acts based on the accepted norm, so it must be true. What other alternatives are there?

The basis for this type of thinking began many centuries ago. For much of our early development as a species we were very vulnerable and without major weapons like sharp teeth, fleet feet, or large, strong bodies. As prey we were driven by fear. In recent centuries, through our ability to work together, our use of tools, and our technology, we have come to dominate the planet. Yet fear is still the prime motivator of our species—fear of survival, fear of each other, fear of death.

The flexibility of our bodies and the creativity of our relatively larger brains are our other major assets. The brain is the body's bio computer and its interpreter of experiences. It constantly calculates the chances of its host's survival as well as optimum situational opportunities for getting comfortable.

Fearful conclusions are reinforced by our parents almost from the moment we take our first breath. At about six years old our mind and ego align and, barring a revelation of some sort in our lifetime, the die is cast, and the grave is the final outcome. Ego reinforces the mind's suspicions and adds its own attempts to dominate, to control the chaos.

Unfortunately, the mind gets bent and twisted by the many influences to which it is subject, day by day--real and imagined occurrences. Most of us have dysfunctional childhoods of one sort or another. These experiences are often assigned false causes, reinforced by strong, negative, emotional reactions to them. Once a theme gets started it is self-fulfilling and has momentum.

The everyday reality I am describing is what I refer to as three-dimensional reality (3d). It sounds pretty grim and uninviting, this life of ours. Yet there is a whole other story to be told.

Five-Dimensional Reality (5D)

The clue to another explanation of reality was hinted at in the third paragraph of Chapter 1, "We arrive here, Souls from the Other Side with high expectations". Here are some of the components of that reality:

- There exists a whole additional dimension, 5D Reality, that is not well known to most, but which is the container in which 3d reality occurs--the life force that animates it.

Awakening to 5D reality is one of our main purposes for coming to Earth and is a blessed event.

- We are Eternal Beings which inhabit a biomechanical vehicle, who have existed since the Beginning and will continue into Infinity.

- This Reality, which our Master Teachers (Jesus, Buddha, Mohammed, Lao Tzu, the Rishis and others too numerous to mention) have tried to show us, exists in an Intelligent Universe of Spirit that wants us to be safe, happy, loving, self-actualized and conscious of our status as Beings with a Higher Consciousness.

- This is a Reality that can be only perceived and lived in by direct experience, rather than with thought and dogma. Meditation is one path to this direct experience.

- Perception of 5D Reality requires a shift in consciousness and contact with our Soul, or individual Higher Consciousness.

- We have other senses with which to perceive Five-Dimensional Reality that must be discovered, since most of us don't know about them or naturally use them.

- Oneness, love, light, joy, peace, health, and abundance are the attributes of this Reality, and are available to us all.

- S/he who achieves Higher Consciousness wins, for the good of the Universe.

Higher Consciousness Meditation is one method to acquaint us with Higher Consciousness and to develop an awareness of this state. To become Aware is a radical shift, mind you, one in which we see ourselves, others and our world from a vastly different perspective.

To accomplish this shift the little self, our 3d body/ mind/ personality has to move over and allow Higher Consciousness to be the focus of awareness. In the end our body/mind/personality is willing to do this, reluctantly, because it recognizes that survival is more likely under these circumstances. It can then do what it was designed to do, receive the plan from Fifth-Dimensional thinking, and to carry it out the plan, propelled by elevated awareness. Our recognition of, and the development of our understanding of Higher Consciousness will make it possible to survive and thrive through what will be seen in the future as a key period of human and planetary evolution.

If/when we are individually and collectively able to make the shift in consciousness, the Garden of Eden will flower forth and we will once again walk and talk with the Father (our personal Higher Consciousness). Alternatively, taking the other, lower, present day path will not be pretty and may result in the relocation of Earthlings from this planet to new planets on which to continue our Soul's journey as Earth becomes uninhabitable.

We only have to look at the lessons from the coronavirus to see how intertwined we are. We are all World Citizens subject to the same dis-eases everywhere as human. Poor leadership and lack for foresight regarding this, and the looming Climate Crisis, will be very painful for mankind if allowed to continue.

For an additional view of the difference between 3-dimensional reality and 5-Dimensional Reality turn to Appendix A. in which I apply this thinking to some of the details of my life.

Why Meditate?

One of the key teachings from our Master Teachers that describes

Fifth Dimensional Reality is the idea that, first, there is an intelligent, unifying force in the Universe (Spirit, God, Divine Intelligence) and that, second, that force resides inside of us. Meditation is one of the ways used by many spiritual traditions to get in touch that force that lies within and is one way to have direct contact with the Divine.

Meditation is equivalent to "silent prayer" in the Christian and other religions. It is a form of prayer that involves listening rather than speaking. Listening for the "Still Small Voice" of God that Elijah reported hearing rather than speaking "at" God and/or asking Him for something.

'Spirit Within' has been taught for thousands of years, well before there was a system for writing the teachings down and continues to be taught today. The following examples illustrate this idea.

For millennia Hindus have acknowledged each other with the greeting *"Namaste"*, meaning *"The Divine in Me Salutes the Divine in You!"* which one commentator expanded upon in this way:

> *I honor the Spirit in you, which is also in me.*
> *I salute the God within you.*
> *Your spirit and my spirit are ONE.*
> *That which is of God in me greets that which is of God in you.*
> *The Divinity within me perceives and adores the Divinity within you.*

One of their earliest holy books, the Upanishads, dating back as far as 1000 BC, states, "The spirit down here in man and the spirit up there in the sun, in reality are only one spirit, and there is no other one."

Lau Tzu, or Laozi, in the first lines of the <u>Tao Te Ching</u>, states that the Tao, God, Spirit is nameless, goes beyond distinctions, and transcends language:

> *The Tao that can be spoken is not the eternal Tao*
> *The name that can be named is not the eternal name*
> *The nameless is the origin of Heaven and Earth*
> *The named is the mother of myriad things*

He goes on to say that this Nameless lies within us:

> *The Valley Spirit never dies*
> *It is named the Mysterious Female.*
> *And the doorway of the Mysterious Female*
> *Is the base from which Heaven and Earth sprang?*
> *It is there within us all the while;*
> *Draw upon it as you will; it never runs dry.*

Responding to a question from the Pharisees about when the Kingdom of God would come, Jesus of Nazareth said, "*The kingdom of God does not come with observation; nor will they say, 'See here!' or 'See there!' For indeed, the kingdom of God is within you*" (Luke 17:20-21). This is yet another acknowledgement of the invisible nature of "God" and his Kingdom as well as the location of that Kingdom within each of us.

He also indicated "...*Your heavenly Father knows that you need all these things (food, drink, clothing). But seek first His kingdom and His righteousness, and all these things will be added to you."...* "*So do not worry about tomorrow; for tomorrow will care for itself. Each day has enough trouble of its own.*"

Mohammed said "*Thou art a mortal being, And thou art the Eternal One; Know thyself, through the light of wisdom. Except Thee there exists none.* "In this statement he acknowledges the duality of all of us as mortal, three dimensional beings and as one with the Eternal. He also said that "*Whoever walks one step towards the grace of Allah (Oneness), the Divine mercy walks forward ten steps to receive him*", indicating that that Oneness will respond immediately to any sign of acknowledgement from us in Its direction.

Siddhartha Gautama Buddha, the one most people think of as the Buddha, in his first sermon, after his famous evening under a Bodhi tree, said "*This Dhamma (Dharma) (understanding of cosmic law and order) (Enlightenment) that I have attained is profound, hard to see and hard to understand, peaceful and sublime, unattainable by mere reasoning, subtle, to be experienced by the wise. It is hard to see this truth, namely the stilling of all formations, the relinquishing of all attachments, the destruction of craving, dispassion, cessation, Nibbana (dis-enchantment)*". This understanding occurred in a profound night of meditation in which he became conscious of the meaning of all phenomena and cause.

From this century come similar statements, one from the Hindu guru Ramana, "*The ordinary man lives in the brain unaware of himself in the Heart. The enlightened one lives in the Heart.*

When he moves about and deals with people and things, he knows that what he sees is not separate from the one Supreme Reality which he realized in the Heart as his own Self."

Carl Jung said it this way, *"Who looks outside, dreams; who looks inside, awakes."*

There are many of other statements from other Master Teachers, famous in their own right, who say essentially the same sorts of things. They form the foundation for the ideas in this book.

The answer to the question, "Why meditate?" then, is that meditation can be used to get in touch with this "One Spirit" and

grow, and evolve us into beings of Higher Consciousness-- making it possible for us to live from a state of greater awareness, of Oneness. Then we can live as the Master Teachers did, with magnificence, as bearers of unconditional love and wisdom, illumined with the Light of the Spirit of the All, and worthy of receiving "all that will be added" to us. We will evolve from homo sapien to Homo Spiritus.

Higher Consciousness

The true Self, Higher Consciousness, has also been referred to as "Christ Consciousness", "Buddha Mind", "Enlightenment" and is within us all, waiting to be discovered. It's the Soul. I affectionately use the term "HiC" for the Beingness that resides inside of me. He (I'm going to use "He" for myself as a male, although "It" is a more proper title) is my true Soul mate. He is the state of consciousness with which my personality is learning to be One.

"Christ Consciousness" or "Christ" is a "title" like teacher, guru, doctor, Mister/Miz. It is a title given to people who have certain abilities or qualities--Blessing qualities, Healing qualities, a quality of Peacefulness, Compassion, Insight, the ability to Communicate in a more conscious way. It comes from having reached a band or level of personal vibration that can be assigned such a title. The label is not the thing. The Thing is the label.

Krishna, Jesus, Buddha, Mohammed, Lao Tzu, and others reached this level of awareness in their lifetimes on planet Earth. They were/are not gods, however, removed from the rest of us. They were simply more evolved beings.

One way to view this is that we are all on a spectrum of consciousness, from very unconscious to highly conscious individuals, worthy of being called "Emily Christ" or "Steve Christ". For those on the unconscious end of the spectrum, Christ Consciousness, for all intents and purposes, doesn't exist. Not in any real way. It's in a state of unrealized potential. Our human selves gradually move from one end of the spectrum to the other over many lifetimes.

Each one of the historical figures mentioned above, whose stories we know so well, had a moment of awakening. We all will have a similar experience, sooner or later, in this lifetime or another. Somewhere, sometime, each of us will take the first, tentative, step on the Path, the Path to Self-realization. Somewhere, sometime, each of us will become Enlightened.

Why Have We Missed the Message?

The comic tragedy is that Higher Consciousness is what our Advanced Teachers have been trying to tell us about for centuries. However, we thought they were saying something else. We turned their teachings into dogma, 3d concepts, and religions. We perverted their teachings because we couldn't understand them with our ego/personality minds. These teachings undermined the very existence of the body/mind/personality and, certainly, its stranglehold over our perceptions.

The essence of the Teachings has been discarded by denial-- "Enlightenment might have been true for Buddha (to name just one) and sounds great, but that could only apply to him. I could never be like that, not really." This relegates what Buddha said, and his life example, as being beyond the average human, beyond the capability of rest of us. Our misunderstanding keeps us from realizing that the Nirvana that he spoke of is only the lifting of a veil which shrouds our clouded eyes.

5-Dimensional Reality describes a model of reality that might, eventually, make obsolete the "agreements" we all share about 3d reality—a paradigm shift of epic proportions. The exploration of 5D reality that is described in this book is just such a paradigm shift. If, in fact, 5D Reality interpenetrates 3d reality and infuses it, the old model will become obsolete. If Higher Consciousness is realizable by all of us, as I maintain that it will be, Heaven on Earth becomes an important possible outcome for our species.

Your, My, Our Futures

This alternative model of reality is what the mystics and Christed Beings have been talking about, each in their own way:

the Garden of Eden, Nirvana, Paradise, Enlightenment, Resurrection, the World to Come. They have attempted to take the blinders off our hypnotized eyes. Each has exhorted us to transcend our small view of reality for the grander reality they were able to see with their inner senses, in their exploration of the transcendent world of 5-Dimensions. This Reality is perceptible, but with different tools than our five human senses, and our limited view of the world as a dangerous and fearful place.

The tools of perception are the same ones our advanced brothers and sisters themselves used: going Within, long enough and deep enough to experience what's there, making contact with Infinity, seeing and sensing a different way, and a change in consciousness. The tools are the "spiritual senses" that we all possess, have at our disposal, but haven't been taught to use. (See Chapter 7 for a description of these Sacred Senses and their use.)

How to Get "There"

How to get There is what this book, and its companion volume, Six Second Mindfulness Meditations, are all about: the tools and methods anybody can use to get There. It's a great adventure for those of us who choose to follow the original pioneers into the new territory, to settle it and make it ours; to develop a more conscious "new normal".

Once the first step has been taken, there's no going back, even if we don't take another step in this lifetime. It's a step for the Ages. Heaven rejoices: "Another Soul has Awakened." Eternity lights up, becomes a little brighter. If you pursue this

Path this time around, then "Wahoo" to you. Much growth can occur. The sky's the limit.

We can become Illumined in this lifetime, depending on how skillful we are at negotiating the Path, how rapidly we can raise our vibration through whatever spiritual practice we undertake. Not that we won't struggle and experience hard times until we've grown sufficiently. However, learning to "go Within" daily can be extremely helpful in coping with our daily lives as well as our Soul's eternal journey. Making contact with our own Higher Consciousness through meditation is, in my opinion, the most direct route.

One of the principals of the Higher Consciousness Meditation process which I advocate (see Chapter 6) is that it is possible to get into a state of being where we feel lit up, illumined, by the glow of Higher Consciousness within. Here's a notation from my meditation journal: "I follow a sequence of steps until Higher Consciousness is reached. My awareness, at one with my HiC, rises to a state of vibration that seems elevated to an unusual degree. At that point, my awareness makes a small leap of recognition. 'I'm yours' I say to my HiC, followed by an additional feeling of 'rising up', an opening up in the brow, a sense of connectedness. Breathing becomes deeper and smoother. Energy seems to pour through me from HiC outward into Eternity."

Questions to Consider

Have you always had the sense that you and your world are more than the obvious; that you have an additional dimension to yourself and that 3d reality is not all there is to life? Describe your understanding.

What's been your experience of being "indoctrinated" into a limited three-dimensional world?

Who was the Master Teacher of your spiritual upbringing? What do you think now after reading this chapter?

What are your spiritual intentions for yourself in this lifetime?

CHAPTER 5

What is Traditional Meditation and What is Higher Consciousness Meditation (HCM)?

Traditional Meditation

The *Miriam-Webster Dictionary* defines meditation as "the act or process of spending time in quiet thought. Continuous and profound contemplation or musing on a subject or series of subjects of a deep or abstruse nature; 'the habit of meditation is the basis for all real knowledge'" (unattributed).

Wikipedia does a better job in its definition of meditation:

> Meditation is a practice in which an individual trains the mind or induces a mode of consciousness, either to realize some benefit or as an end in itself.

> The term "meditation" (much like the term "sports") refers to a broad variety of practices that includes techniques designed to promote relaxation, build internal energy or life force (*qi, ki, prana,* etc.) and develop

compassion, love, patience, generosity and forgiveness. A particularly ambitious form of meditation aims at effortlessly sustained single-pointed concentration meant to enable its practitioner to enjoy an <u>indestructible sense of well-being</u> while engaging in any life activity.

The word *meditation* carries different meanings in different contexts. Meditation has been practiced since antiquity as a component of numerous religious traditions and beliefs. Meditation often involves an internal effort to self-regulate the mind in some way. Meditation is often used to clear the mind and ease many health issues, such as <u>high</u> <u>blood pressure</u>, <u>depression</u>, and <u>anxiety</u>. It may be done while sitting, or in an active way. For instance, <u>Buddhist monks</u> (and others, ed.) involve awareness (called "mindfulness", ed.) in their day-to-day activities as a form of mind-training. <u>Prayer beads</u> or other ritual objects are commonly used during meditation in order to keep track of or remind the practitioner about some aspect of the training.

Among the ideas expressed in these definitions and in the Wikipedia commentary that I think are salient:

- Meditation has been used for centuries to quieten the mind until thoughts cease for short or extended periods of time or to "induce a mode of consciousness" that, in spiritual traditions, brought the meditator closer to God or generated a heightened spiritual state. Meditation has been more often employed by the mystical forms of our familiar spiritual traditions, the Kabbalist form of Judaism, Yoga in Hinduism, Sufism in Islam, and Christian Hesychasm.

- The story of Gautama Buddha and his awakening is the one most directly tied to meditation. Enlightenment through meditation came after he spent years of exploring numerous spiritual traditions and studying with many different teachers in India.

- In Buddhist meditation the spiritual goal is to reach a state of Nirvana, an elevated state of awareness which very few who attempt this approach manage to achieve. Those who do get there are thought of, and revered, as enlightened.

- Traditional meditation is difficult because it assumes that the mind is a wild horse that needs to be tamed and uses sitting quietly, observing one's thoughts, and being aware of one's breath as its process. Sometimes, meditation incorporates the repeating of mantras (sacred words) and/or the use of objects (beads, a rosary, etc.) to self-regulate and/or subdue the mind. Unfortunately, such an approach often takes years and years of practice to be successful; to tame that wild horse is not easy.

- I have been meditating for over 45 years, beginning at Swami Sachidananda's Integral Yoga Institute in San Francisco, and have explored a number of other traditions. I have found that the methods I tried are something of a quest--an engagement with my mind until it began to quieten down a little, and then more and more. I experienced it as a wrestling match, and many others have said the same thing, to take that wild horse that is the mind and tame it. This is difficult and many people quit before ever getting there. It's hard. Worthwhile, for sure, but tough for most of us.

- Meditation has been used increasingly in the West for secular purposes, for the scientifically proven benefits it grants—including the easing of health issues, such "high blood pressure, depression, and anxiety" as mentioned above.

- Joh Kabat-Zinn, founder of the Mindfulness-Based Stress Reduction program in the late '70s, has shown scientifically that his practice increases the body's ability to heal and includes a shift from a tendency to use the right prefrontal cortex instead of the left prefrontal cortex. This shift is associated with a trend away from depression and anxiety and towards happiness, relaxation, and emotional balance.

Mindfulness induces a state of "moment to moment non-judgmental awareness" using, among other things, thought and breath observation, body scanning, mindful walking and being aware of the taste and texture of the food that we eat. It's a way, with acute observation, to quieten the mind and allow 5D consciousness to flow into 3d situations.

Higher Consciousness Meditation (HCM)

HCM builds on traditional meditation and is, in my opinion, the next step in the evolution of meditation as well as human evolution. HCM is built around a process that is simple, straightforward, but very powerful. In addition, HCM offers a variety of other forms, triggers and tricks that add to the process' effectiveness and offers variety to keep the practice interesting. Some of you may find that the core process does not suit you and that some of the other forms, triggers and tricks are more to your liking. Whatever works for you works for me.

How you use what is offered here is up to you. Adapt it, vary it, experiment. You may find that you like some methods better in the beginning and others later as you develop your personal practice. If none of it works, set it aside for now.

Confer with your Higher Consciousness, your sacred place within, for guidance. If you are like me you've known for many years that you have a Higher Consciousness, a Soul, but just didn't know how to access that part of yourself in a deep and satisfying way. As for me, I remember reading about my Thought Adjustor in the Urantia Book many years ago and my heart leapt with recognition. However, it was not until recently, 35 years later, that I began to develop a deep relationship with that part of myself through the Higher Consciousness Meditation process that I will show you below.

If you let it, the process will lead you to an **experience,** an experience of your own Higher Consciousness and the higher vibration associated with this experience. This experience is hard to describe and is unique to each individual. However, the process will allow you to experience Yourself in all of your magnificence, the magnificence that comes when Spirit flows into and through your human, three dimensional limitations, and expands you into Five-Dimensional Reality.

Questions to consider:

What has been your experience of with meditation (or contemplative prayer)? What struggles have you had, and progress have you made?

What is your initial reaction to the idea of Higher Consciousness Meditation? Does it seem worth pursuing?

CHAPTER 6.

The Higher Consciousness Meditation Process

Higher Consciousness Meditation is, as I have said, a process. A process with preparations to make and steps to take. It is not a formula, however. Your experience is likely be new and fresh each time, fueled by your own Higher Consciousness. You may experience this Higher Consciousness as a state of elevated awareness, or as that higher form of yourself, your Soul, who is like an older, wiser brother or sister. Use the process, and the other forms offered here, but do not become too hung up on the details. Let it take you where it takes you.

Begin by deciding that experiencing your Higher Consciousness is something you really want to do and that you are willing to put in the time and effort to make it happen. Whether you are a beginner or an expert meditator, there is no way you can mess it up. It will work because it's on your Soul's line of purpose if you do. Soul is ready. Always.

HCM is easier to do than traditional meditation because the practice is not a wrestling match with the mind. Instead, your 3d body/mind/personality, your normal state of awareness, will probably resist some but will eventually begin to engage in the process and be willing to give up control, at least some of the time, for the benefits HCM provides.

Getting Started: Choose a Comfortable Time, Comfortable Place; Equipment

Higher Consciousness Meditation (HCM) can be done once a day for 6 minutes or less and gain the benefit. Furthermore, HCM can be done for hours at a time and still be a ton of fun. I typically meditate for 20-30 minutes in the morning without strain and for 10-15 minutes before going to bed. Sometimes I get There in 30 seconds, and don't even have to do the process. It is fair to say that I have been meditating off and on for a long time, with varying degrees of success. Anything longer than 20 minutes, though, was previously a strain until recently.

Although any time is good, select a specific time every day to meditate if you can. I like to meditate in the morning at about 6:30 after feeding our herd of three animals and doing about 15 minutes of yoga. I have found that HCM is a wonderful way to start the day, in a higher vibratory frame of mind.

I like getting up early when no one else is up and the house is quiet. Find a time that works for you. Experiment. Just do it. If possible, do it twice a day for 6 minutes, in the morning and at night before retiring, to amplify the experience.

One of the major benefits of HCM, your ability to increase your vibratory rate, will make this lifetime a much better experience. In addition, if you are a strategic thinker like I am, you will come to realize that you are probably going to reincarnate back to Earth over and over, and that doing this work/play now will make your life(s) much better over the course of Eternity.

Meditation is best done seated on the floor, in a cross-legged posture, or when sitting comfortably in a straight-backed chair. I usually sit on the floor on the yoga mat I just finished using (in the morning), on a meditation cushion. I never have been limber enough to assume a full "lotus position" (see Google for "lotus position"). Instead, I sit cross-legged with wrists resting on my knees, and fingers extended, except for the first finger and thumb which are curled and touching. This gives me a good, balanced position to be in for a while.

The alternative is to sit in an upright chair with uncrossed arms and legs. Put your feet flat on the floor, parallel to each other, and rest the hands on the knees. Lastly, if you are so inclined, meditate in the bathtub, as my wife Lynne likes to do.

In any case, make it as easy as possible (except for the tub approach) to sit up straight, comfortably. (By the way, I find that an easy chair is "too easy" to relax into and to begin to nod off.) If you find yourself nodding off, shift your place or way of sitting. Keep in mind that nodding off may be a form of resistance on the part of the body/mind/personality to participating in a threatening activity. Initially, it may push back a bit and attempt to thwart your intentions to Wake Up. This will dissipate in short order of you keep doing the Sacred Breaths mentioned later. They will dissolve the resistance. And get enough sleep if you are sleeping too little. Sleep deprivation is very widespread and spoils my meditation if I don't get enough sleep.

Step by Step Sequence for a 6 Minute HCM Meditation

- Begin by taking three deep breaths, each one a little deeper than the first one. Each time let the breath out slowly using your diaphragm to finish the exhale with a little push.
- Then say to yourself, "Peace, Be Still" (one of the most powerful sayings ever. Use it anytime you think to do so.) Say the words slowly and get the significance of each one individually, as well as together. "Peace". "Be". "Still".
- Take another deep breath; this time thinking of it as a Sacred Breath (you can feel the difference as your rate of vibration begins to increase). Let it out slowly.
- Then say to yourself, "The ALL (or God) is....." and let this be an open-ended statement. Sometimes these two words are a sufficiently long statement to get a sense of Spirit's Presence, a sense of The ALL—Eternity. Other times the statement wants to finish itself, with... "Source" or "One with me" or whatever bubbles up. Lately, the phrase has been a statement-- "The ALL Is." Followed by either "I am The ALL unfolding and unfolding" or "Love The ALL. Be The ALL."

(The goal is to get, however slightly, the feeling of Omnipresence or Allness. This has a very distinct vibration to it and is available to you if you just reach out, or, more properly said, let It in. Or even better let your Within expand out to fill It. This is true of the whole meditation exercise--you are seeking to allow your vibration to increase by tapping into your Higher

Consciousness. The more you do it the stronger the feeling gets, and for longer periods of time.)

Sometimes "The ALL Is...." is all I have to say to feel transported into a state of Higher Consciousness. Sometimes there is a tangible sense of Omnipresence, one of Spirit's attributes--a feeling of being One with All of It. This is an experience that I can just melt into and enjoy like eating a never-ending ice cream cone--an all-encompassing moment of Eternal Now. Sometimes gratitude wells up; a "thank you" for the moment of "Wow". Sometimes, I am so in the Now that the moment seems to last forever.

Finish off by saying "I am one with That".

- Take another Sacred Breath and enjoy the experience.
- Then say to yourself, "My Higher Consciousness (or God Within) is....."--again an open-ended statement where you open to sensing your Higher Consciousness. Sometimes the statement finishes itself. Everything from "...my buddy", to "....my Eternal Companion", "....individualized Spirit" or "....filling me up" have been sentence completions that have come through me.

Allow yourself to sense the Presence--to "feel" It. Search inside of you for the feeling of this Presence. It is there, and your Soul wants you to perceive It/Him/Her; to establish contact. Allow yourself to be imbued with it. Savor it. This Presence that will seem remarkably familiar, normal, yet at a vibratory that might be called "ephemeral". This is You, at your finest. The real You. The Eternal You. The You that you know you Are but can't even begin to express in hidebound language. Through making this contact, you are establishing your own unique, one-of-a-kind Partnership for the Ages.

Again, say to yourself, "I am one with That".

- Take another Sacred Breath or two. Experience the Experience.
- Then say to yourself, "I Am......" your third open ended statement. This, for me, is often followed by ....."an Eternal Being. Or "I am Eternity Being". Other times "...Awake and Aware", "...One with The ALL, and One with my Higher Consciousness".

Your "Youness" craves union with Spirit, with The ALL, and with your Higher Consciousness more than life itself, because it is Life Itself. How can Three (The ALL, your HiC, and Eternal Being) be One? That's the magic of the mystical experience that we are all destined for.

- (These statements are meant to open you up for the expansion of Spirit. In the beginning you may get "nothing", or you may get "something" that is hard to describe. If you get something, you may doubt that it is really coming from the realm of Spirit and not your mind. Do this process for a week or so. You'll know. It will begin to build into something trustworthy.)
- Then take three more Sacred Breaths. With each one feel Spirit's energy expanding within you. Each time pause just a second to let the energy pool up in your heart. Then exhale slowly, feeling Spirit energy radiating from you out into your world. Your exhale

may be as much as twice as long as the inhale, but don't strain to try to do this.

- At this point, I just enjoy the feeling of touching Five-Dimensional Reality. I often have an experience of profound well-being, of Spirit surrounding and infusing me. I may have a conversation with my Higher Consciousness, my HiC. This might take the form of a question like "HiC, what do you want from me?", or "What can you tell me about this?" related to some issue or occurrence I may be experiencing in my life. Or I may simply let myself be filled with Spirit for a time.
- At the end of your available time say the following:
  - "Thank you Spirit for this time together"
  - "May your light and love fill my world this day"
- Take several more Sacred Breaths and come out of the meditation.
- Stretch, stand, and reflect for a moment on the experience. If you have time, make a few notes in your meditation journal, if you have one.
- Put your yoga mat and cushion away if you are using them.
- Move on to your next activity. Allow this elevated sense of Awareness to stay with you for as long as you can. Remember to come back to it throughout the day.

Pretty simple, but immensely powerful. An ideal outcome would be reaching a State in which you are calm and comfortable and can feel yourself glowing with the level of higher vibration you have reached. The process can easily be done in 6 minutes although 10 minutes is better if you have the time, so as to not feel rushed. And to have a moment or two to relax into your Higher Consciousness at the end. If you have a more time just continue the Sacred Breath sequence.

It only takes doing the process a few times to get the hang of it. Use a 3x5 card to make a "cheat sheet" of the steps if that is helpful. Before long, the sequence becomes second nature and the quality of the Breaths become stronger.

Please don't feel that you must do HCM exactly as presented. This is not a formula but a detailed outline. Follow it long enough to get a good sense of it, to begin having experiences of your vibratory rate increasing, and make it your own. This is adult learning by experience. Allow yourself to be creative and to just "go with the flow" of where Spirit takes you.

What you are looking for is your path to your Higher Consciousness. Better said, you are opening yourself for It to expand in you, which It is ready to do as soon as you quieten down and turn in Its direction. The meditation is intended to do that. Spirit will flood you as soon as you will allow It to. It's been waiting lifetimes for you to open to It. Spirit will expand and cause you to "light up". Spirit will then flow out into your world to accomplish Its purposes, one of which is to dramatically improve your sense of wellbeing by attracting favorable things and experiences into your life.

This process is how I do most of my meditations. I love the feeling of a vibratory rate increase--the sign of a shift in consciousness up to the 5D level, and a common occurrence in Higher Consciousness Meditation. I also love the sense of the Presence of my personal Higher Consciousness, and the conversations I have with Him from time to time. These days, it is not uncommon for me to meditate for between 20 and 30 minutes at a time and the time seems to go by quickly. (Stop, by the way, if/whenever you feel uncomfortable, physically, mentally, or emotionally.)

The benefit of this type of practice is multiplied if you meditate for 6-10 minutes twice a day. Do the process a second time on your meditation cushion or as you lie down to go to sleep—it will pervade your slumber and you will have better dreams. Don't worry if you go to sleep before you finish. If you wake up in the middle of the night, take a series of Sacred Breaths until you fall back to sleep.

Don't extend your HCM sessions beyond 10 minutes unless it does not cause you strain. This is supposed to be relaxing and fun. Spend more time if and when it feels good and refreshing to do so.

If you're interested in exploring my yoga mat and meditation cushion preferences, go to my web site for more information.

In the next few chapters I will offer some additional meditation forms along with tricks and triggers to enhance your Unfolding.

Questions to Consider:

What do you think about the Higher Consciousness Meditation Process as outlined?

If you have tried it a time or two what is your experience?

What questions or concerns do you have about it?

Chapter 7.

Sacred Senses

I have already described one of the 7 Sacred Senses I will discuss in this chapter, the Sacred Breath, and its use in the Higher Consciousness Meditation process. Sacred Senses are a higher consciousness form of our physical senses and can be used to help us achieve a state of Elevated Awareness, and increase our vibration, if only for a moment. The sacred use of our physical senses to elevate our state of consciousness can be done quickly, can enliven our day, and can propel us into a more illumined state of personal awareness.

The key to taking advantage of our Sacred Senses is remembering to remember to use them. While this may sound odd; it is not. The elevated state of awareness that we experience in HCM is extremely attractive. It is really our true state of being. I would love to be in this state all the time. I'm happier, sharper, more intuitive, and more fun to be with when I am more conscious.

However, my state of Higher Consciousness achieved during meditation inevitably "wears off" as my morning unfolds.

Sometimes something catches my attention and pulls me into its "realm", its vibration. If I have to get out on the freeway, the demands of that activity are very compelling and I forget my elevated state as my normal, everyday 3d consciousness takes over and drives me to my destination.

Fortunately, I now know that I have another option, but I have to remember to remember to exercise that set of muscles. Like any new skill, it has to be used. Like any new set of learnings, it takes a while to master them and have them become our "new normal". Developing and using our Sacred Senses can help elevate consciousness and is intrinsically rewarding just in the doing.

Also, keep in mind that each of us prefers the use of the 5 senses in normal, everyday life. Some people are more visually oriented and will say "I see what you are saying" instead of "I hear what you are saying", revealing a personal sense preference for seeing rather than hearing. Consider your personal preference and "see" if you like some or one of the Sacred Senses more than the others.

Some of the examples offered below are meditative practices and some are mindfulness practices, as you will see in the methods and examples presented. Meditation and mindfulness practices are often two sides of the same coin.

Sacred Seeing

Sacred Seeing is one of the most powerful ways we can use to raise our consciousness. Sacred Seeing involves more than the typical way to see by taking in and processing visual information. Shifting into a higher state of awareness with seeing can be done in these ways:

- See the Soul, or Higher Self in others. This is a big one for me, so I will spend some extra time on it. My 3d mind has a strong proclivity to be judge, jury and executioner. Not so awfully long ago I slowed down long enough to recognize how pervasive is my need, desire, compulsion to judge everyone I meet. I still catch my body/mind/personality making up stories about everything I see. "That car means this person is well-to-do, a go-getter." "That old Pontiac Lemans means that person is only able to afford an old car with dents. He "should" fix those dents" ("should" is a word my body/mind/personality uses quite a bit). "That person looks like someone who doesn't care about his health, has no discipline to keep himself fit, and should do something about it."

Crazy stuff; stuff swimming around at such a low level of consciousness that it's embarrassing to acknowledge the truth of it. At least now, however, I have slowed down enough to notice what kinds of thoughts are flowing through my brain, and to look Within to ask "Well, what is that all about?" Of course, the answer is, "3d mind at work". The 3d mind is a judging mind, a discriminating mind, a justifying mind, a mind that makes things up when faced with a lack of information. Well, that's not exactly right. In reality, my mind makes things up all of the time. Rain or shine. It makes others "wrong" to make myself and my ways "right" --neuron firings to justify my behavior and the quirks of my personality.

o Sacred Seeing is the blessed antidote to mental judgment. I have been practicing with Lynne as we sit in the evening, having a glass of wine and debriefing the day. I see her in all of her magnificence, and it moves me. My vibration shoots up.

o I also practice Sacred Seeing when I go to the grocery store.
Here's the technique: Take a Sacred Breath. Squint a little and soften your eyes. Look to see if you can see the Christ in those around you. Even for just a flash.

It works. When I am successful, my mind shifts up to the 5th Dimension and I can see people's auras. I see them from a loving perspective, am in a gentle state, acknowledge them with a smile, and the whole store seems to light up.

• Sacred Seeing allows us to take in more, relevant, intuitional information about something of which we might not, otherwise, be aware. For example, I can look at a plant outside of the house with Sacred Eyes and see its state of health—its need for water, its need for sunshine, whether its location is favorable, or it needs to be moved. Lynne has taught me this with her power of non-judgmental seeing, one of her strengths about people and things.

Using this one technique, alone, could cause anyone to become illumined in this lifetime, if we can perfect it and "see" all things and people around us this way.

This evening, for example, I was petting our beloved Annie Cat. All at once, I shifted into a different valence of "seeing", and "saw" that I was petting myself. That I was not body limited but had shifted into seeing my immediate surroundings as "me" and my Oneness with It (my surroundings). This is what true compassion must be, a sense of Oneness in which all is well, and all is beloved and the object of my attention is Sacred.

Sacred Tasting/Smelling/Eating

If you're like me, you tend to eat too fast and don't enjoy your food enough. Sacred Tasting (and Smelling) is so important to the enjoyment, consumption, and processing of food.

- I first became aware of the notion of Sacred Tasting at the Integral Yoga Institute in San Francisco in 1975. Lynne and I took a vegetarian cooking class there on Saturday mornings for several months. The class would prepare lunch for ourselves and for the staff, about 15 people.

  We ate together in silence, the first time I had ever heard of doing such a thing. Called mindful eating, the practice was done in silence and we were to take one bite, put down our fork, and chew until the last swallow before taking another bite. It took a while longer than usual to eat, granted, but I learned to savor the food, pay attention to its smells, distinguish various spices, notice the texture of the ingredients, and eat peacefully.

- Over the years I had abandoned the practice of paying that type of attention to my food until recently. With my deepening meditation practice and with Lynne's urging, I am relearning not to bolt down my food and pay more attention, to be more aware, of the loveliness of what I am eating.

- In my research I have found nutritionists say that this technique helps people to lose weight. This makes sense to me as I am much more aware of when I have had an "ample sufficiency", as my father-in-law used to say, and thereby avoid eating too much because of the inertia of eating too fast. I also think that I sometimes have engaged in "emotional eating" --taking in too much food when I am emotionally agitated. Mindful eating can help with this tendency, as well.

- The Zen Buddhist teacher, Thich Nat Hahn, speaks this way of drinking tea, which also applies to eating and any other mindfulness practice, "Drink your tea slowly and reverently, as if it is the axis on which the world earth revolves--slowly, evenly, without rushing toward the future. Live the actual moment. Only this moment is life."

- Our vegetarian cooking class also introduced us to the idea that being in a peaceful state of mind is important for the cook. Not only did we eat in silence, but we also prepared the food in respectful silence as well. Our teacher, Swami Nirmalananda, more than once reminded us of the importance of not being agitated or upset when we were in the kitchen. (Lynne and I were in a difficult time in our relationship and sometimes we would bring that energy to the Saturday morning class.) She said that if we were upset we would cook that into the food and give our diners indigestion. She was a saint to put up with us the way she did. Thanks Swami. We made it!

- Lastly, Lynne and I have become more and more conscious over the years about the quality and type of food we eat. We go to the farmer's market as much as possible to get organic fruit and vegetables, and organic meats at the grocery story. Our typical evening meal is an entrée and a salad, sometimes with frozen yogurt to top it off.

Recently we began experimenting with a style of cooking called Ayurveda. It's an ancient Hindu practice based on several ideas:

- The way food is prepared can be healing in nature as well as healthy. The courses, the ingredients, and the spices can be selected in such a way as to promote overall health as well as to target particular health conditions so as to promote the healing of those conditions. We have been using The Ayurveda Cookbook by Amadea Morningstar, which also talks quite a bit about the philosophy behind the practice.

We won't use this system exclusively; we may use the recipes once or twice a week. Conceptually, the approach makes sense, though. We have also experimented with putting chicken or shrimp in her recipes as we are not vegetarians. This has worked quite well.

- Ayurveda also uses the Hindu concept of personality types and the importance of matching up the type of food and ingredients to your personality type. (There is a little profile quiz to determine your personality type if you want to pursue this idea at https://www.theaurvedaexperience.com/dosha-quiz/).

People, like the two of us, who are "Pita" types (tending toward being fiery, strong willed and determined) should avoid fried foods, caffeine and hot spices, for example, and emphasize fresh fruit, vegetables, milk products and whole grains.

Sacred Touching

- There are a number of practices that we can undertake to touch with exquisiteness. There is nothing like the feel of a baby's skin, snow, alpaca fabric, the seams of a baseball, bird feathers, a heating pad, soft lips, and more. Being mindful of the feel of the world around us helps bring us into the "here and now"--to be more present and possibly to feel the Presence of Spirit.

- It's possible to enjoy all types of touch sensations when we slow down to pay attention to this sense: texture, hardness, temperature, roughness, aliveness, cleanliness, and more.

- I was recently introduced to the idea of using touch as a way of short-circuiting taught by an on-line tennis teacher, Will Hamilton, at Fuzzy Yellow Balls, and, to a lesser degree, Ian Westerman at Essential Tennis. (I use tennis analogies throughout my writing because I play and because I am applying my principals to playing better and with more enjoyment.) In tennis and golf, it is important to stay calm and relaxed to play well, unlike football where an adrenaline rush can help you tackle harder.

However, when at the end of a set of tennis and I am serving to win the set, it is very easy for my mind to imagine the consequences of winning or blowing it, choking, and cause the adrenaline to begin to flow— sometimes dramatically. The result is that I sometimes tighten up, lose the flow of my serve, and may end up hitting the ball into the net.

Will's sports psychologist friend and fellow teacher, Dr. Marc Kovacs says that the best thing that we can do in that moment is the following:

- o Walk around a bit and feel the ground with your feet
- o Bounce the ball three times and watch it bounce. Feel the fuzz on the ball.
- o Breathe in through the nose and out through the mouth.
- o Feel the texture of the racquet handle. Loosen your grip on the racquet.
- o Watch the seams of the ball rotate as you toss the ball upwards.
- o Extend your arm and keep it up there an extra second instant to stay more upright.

Kovacs maintains that doing these things causes the mind to quieten, since the brain can't process both thought and feeling at the same time. Concentrating on touch shorts out the thoughts and the emotional flow of unwanted adrenaline. Not only do I find that these things work but they are lessons for daily life.

If we are about to get up and give a speech, which most people hate, it can help to take an object from your pocket, perhaps a special stone, and focus on the texture and feel of it. Become aware of the feel of your feet on the floor as you walk to the podium. Touch the podium with interest and feel the texture of the top of it.

There are all kinds of situations to which we can apply this technique when staying calm is the order of the day.

Sacred Hearing

- "Do you hear what I am saying?" is a common plaintive cry of one human to another. While, on one hand, it is impossible to really and truly know fully and completely what another is saying or feeling, we all want to be heard and understood by the important people in our lives. Sacred Hearing or Listening can bridge that gap.

Really "hearing" somebody is an art. Not being "heard" can be excruciatingly frustrating. In my business consulting work at the SBTDC in North Carolina I spent considerable time training our consultants, especially the new ones, to be good, active listeners. This key skill is one few newbies had when they began working with us.

Mirroring back to the client what he or she might have just said was helpful. As was rephrasing their commentary and asking if that is what was meant often clarified an issue. Asking the client to "tell me more about that" helped to drill down into a problem to get at the root cause. It helped us to help clients discover their own answers to problems and issues they were having.

- One key technique that is often used in mindfulness workshops is Sacred Walking--walking slowly and observing as much as possible of what is going within us, and around us, in the process of walking our bodies. The instructions often include "opening our Inner Ear" to hear the symphony of sounds of nature cascading around us.

- Listening to our inner voice, our intuition, or our individual Higher Consciousness, the HiC that I spoke of earlier, is an example of Sacred Listening and Hearing. It has been said that the best form of prayer is one of listening rather than speaking. Offering gratitude for Divinity's gifts rather asking Divinity for more, more, more, as if God were a Santa Claus, can also open those Sacred Ears.

- Sacred music has a higher vibratory rate. Some music is known to have healing properties, including "soothing the savage beast". See the topic Sacred Music below.

Sacred Healing

While healing is not necessarily one of the five senses, I would certainly put Healing into the category of Sacred Senses. I will be brief in my remarks about healing in this book and will have much more to say about that in a future volume.

We all have been wounded physically, emotionally, mentally, and spiritually. Some have been severely wounded in one or more of these areas.   It's part of the human condition that I mentioned earlier, part of the landscape of a material world. If we fall, we skin our knees. Someone screaming at us can leave an emotional scar. Severe traumas can affect us for a whole lifetime if they are not dealt with effectively.

Higher Consciousness Meditation can be helpful to the healing process in a number of ways. First, being in a state of Higher Consciousness generates a higher physical, mental, emotional, spiritual vibration. Higher vibrations tend to ward off illness and to mitigate the frequency and severity of a state of a dis-ease. Many physical conditions are caused by fear and a high-octane lifestyle.

A higher state of vibration can augment the healing properties of a medical procedure or cause a dis-ease to begin to melt away in the sunlight of Spirit. Also, those who are in a state of Higher Consciousness tend to make better choices about their habits and routines, and make choices to avoid lower level vibrational, less healthy activities.

Most of our Master Teachers were said to be superb healers. Spontaneous healings often occurred to those with various afflictions from just being in their presences.   I think this occurred because the atmosphere around them was so charged with higher vibration that dis-eases just melted in the presence of the Teacher's Illumination. Healing benefits are available to those who case raise their internal vibrations through practices like Higher Consciousness Meditation.

As I mentioned earlier, healing will be the in-depth subject of another book, but I would like to mention one use of Sacred Breathing (see below) that I have used recently in certain situations where healing was called for. For example, I have found that if I cut my face shaving, strain a muscle, or bang myself somehow, and I remember to take a mental step back from the trauma of what has just happened to take a Sacred Breath, two things occur. First, I calm myself down more quickly to assess and react better to the situation, and second, the healing process seems to take less time. I think the latter is true because my body goes into a higher state of vibration immediately before the trauma takes over, and that promotes accelerated recovery.

Sacred Breathing

I've saved my favorite subject in the realm of Sacred Senses for last—Sacred Breathing. It may be the most powerful tool we have if we learn how to use it properly, as the follow discussion attests. While Sacred Breathing doesn't have a direct correlation to one of the five physical senses, I think it is the most powerful and versatile of all the Sacred Senses. Sacred Breaths, Christ Breaths, Transcendent Breaths, Healing Breaths, Love Breaths, Forgiveness Breaths, and others are possible and useful. It takes so little for us to pause and take a Breath that has a particular purpose determined by our intent.

Sacred Breaths are certainly a way to raise our consciousness, the vibration of our Being, and they are a key component of the

HCM process described earlier. In summary, a Sacred Breath is taken by expanding the Spirit that lies within all of us into on the inbreath, pausing for a second to let Spirit pool up, and then radiating Spirit out into your world on the outbreath. Doing so enlivens ourselves and the world around us.

Part of the value of Sacred Breathing is that it is a tool to be used repeatedly to soothe our body/mind/personality and help it get comfortable with a "new normal" of Spirit/Mind being in charge, and our systems operating at a higher vibration. I remember when this experience of higher vibration was new to me, intriguing, and a bit scary to my mind as I observed my mind's reaction to the new experience. I liken this to our 8-year-old cat's reaction to the new kitten that recently appeared in our lives. Annie Cat acted intimidated and intimidating with 5-week-old Cleo. She did not like the change and acted very territorial with the little one, hissing and growling and puffing up.

There is no justification for this except that it is Annie's natural reaction to change, much like our human mind when something new is introduced into its system. Slowly Annie learned that there was no threat; that this new creature was harmless. Perhaps, as Lynne speculates, on some level she knew that this was a baby feline, worthy of mothering. Annie got used to the little one and, before long, when we went on a 3-day trip she had company and didn't miss us as much.

In Higher Consciousness Meditation Sacred Breathing is used in the process to help trigger and deepen each step. It can also be used in these ways as well:

- As a quick trigger to raise our vibration any time we use it. Simply say the opening phrase to HCM, "Peace, be still" and take a long, slow breath. This will immediately put us into a different state of mind. It can be used anytime, anywhere. Silently. Nobody else needs to know. I have used this exercise in many different situations. For example, I will take a Sacred Breath just before just about any task: starting a meeting, beginning a difficult conversation, serving a tennis ball. It enriches the moment and puts me into a better frame of mind to accomplish the task.

- As a consciousness shifter while doing a repetitious, frightening, or physical task--digging a ditch, having teeth drilled, or cooking some food. I think my fish always tastes better and has more love cooked into it when I practice Sacred Breathing.

- Subconscious mind breathing
  - We each have a subconscious or unconscious mind--a concept popularized by Sigmund Freud. Since its introduction, empirical evidence suggests that subconscious mind phenomena include repressed feelings, automatic skills, subliminal perceptions, thoughts, habits, automatic reactions, and, possibly, complexes, hidden phobias and desires, and repressed memories of painful incidents.

  - I have found it helpful to breathe into that part of myself that has been agitated by something in my interior or exterior environment. Recently, for example, I woke up with a feeling in the pit of my stomach. Fear. I didn't recognize it at first, thinking it might be indigestion (which I never get). I spent 15 minutes in bed working on dissolving the fear, reaching for some good feelings, using my meditation techniques. Nothing much worked.

I got up, did my usual yoga routine, and spent about twenty minutes in an intense meditation-- really Breathing into the pit of my stomach. The fear began to subside and the "aha" moment came. I had gone to bed without meditating the night before, and after listening to a webinar that ended with the usual "scarcity" scenario; "If you don't buy this product before midnight you will lose out". I wasn't even that interested in the product, a software solution to a problem I didn't have. My subconscious mind, however, had been hooked by the message.

A few more Sacred Breaths and my consciousness began to move in the direction of Awareness. My vibratory rate rose. The fear subsided and was replaced by an eagerness for the day, by a sense of feeling good, by a feeling of lightness. It was with this that I was able to begin the day. Lynne and I went shopping and found some great plants for the yard. I worked in my office for a while and some pieces of a project fell into place. All in all, it was a good day.

I learned long ago to avoid watching scary movies, or anything else that is fear-based, before I go to bed—such input lodges in my subconscious mind and my dreams are often troubled when I do.

o   Lynne pointed out to me that I was speaking to another person in our Tai Chi class in the same overbearing way my father used to use. It never worked for him very well, but I think I learned it from him, and it sometimes comes out in inappropriate ways. That evening I spent a while breathing in a sacred way into that part of me where the behavior was lodged. Since then I have been able to catch myself before launching into that undesirable behavior.

o   One morning a year ago, in meditation, I was inspired. "Breathe me", I said to HiC. "Breathe me and through me. Breathe me and be me. Fill my very lungs with Spirit." I felt the intake of Spirit and the exhale of Spirit, into my world and into Eternity. I thought, "All I have to do is do this and I am filled with Light." It was this incident that led me to include Sacred Breathing as a key part of Higher Consciousness Meditation.

• Some "Quickies" for Sacred Breathing

o   Take a Sacred Breath anytime you think about it. This intentional act is one of the best ways to increase your vibratory rate and to "charge" the atmosphere around you.

o Pause as you go through a door and take a Sacred Breath as you make that transition. We go in and out of doors frequently. The idea is to make an association between one activity (going through a door) and another (taking a Sacred Breath).

Observant Jews take this one step further. Inside a little rectangular case, mounted on the inside front door frame, they hang a Mezuzah-- two chapters from the Torah written on a rolled-up scroll. The first verse is "Hear oh Israel, the L-rd is our G-d, the L-rd is One." When leaving the house, they touch the Mezuzah and remember that God is One. We can borrow from this tradition and put whatever we want on the door frame to touch as a reminder to elevate our consciousness as we leave to go out into the world.

o Prime yourself for good dreams before you go to sleep. Take a series of Sacred Breaths as you snuggle down until you fall asleep. Not only will it be easier to go to sleep, but your dreams will be better. Write them down when you wake up. If you have a bad dream take the opportunity to breathe Sacred Breaths into your subconscious mind to discover what might be learned. Rejoice in the higher vibration dreams you experience.

Questions to Consider

What do you think about the idea that your 5 physical senses have a sacred counterpart to them?

Which ones of these appeal to you the most? Why?

Are you eager to try them out? How and when?

CHAPTER 8

Other Ways to Tap into Higher Consciousness

Virtually any activity can be done in a mindful way, allowing us to enter a state of Higher Awareness and be totally immersed in the immediacy of the moment, into the Now. And the Now. And the Now.

My friend Murugananda, who was one of Sri Satchidananda's closest friends and companions, addressed this idea more eloquently than I ever could in an email he sent to Lynne and me:

"Meditation is not some 2hr/day thing, not just some sitting and turning beads, saying mantras and so on. Meditation is 24/7 mindfulness. Mindfulness - when you eat, when you chew, when you wash hands. Mindfulness, and gratitude too, when you cross the street. Mindfulness when you pee. Mindfulness when you order at a restaurant.

In some traditions, like Zen and Jewish traditions, there are prayers for everything you do - when you awaken in the morning, there is a prayer, a prayer for washing hands before eating, for being able to pee. This is for gratitude and to be aware. This is meditation.

Of course, being able to clear the mind of crap helps a lot - just to realize it's all crap. There is a limit to our time in this body - so waste not in nonsense - realize that you and all things in the Universe are a part of that ONE reality and in fact ARE that - the true God consciousness. There is nothing that you have to attain; you are already that. Thus, endeth the first spontaneous discourse - for what it's worth.

"Spot on good buddy" is what I have to say about that.

Sacred Music, Sacred Songs

Sacred music and sacred songs have been used since people began to gather around fires and imagine themselves as being more than two-legged creatures trying to eat and keep from being eaten. Such music has been used to scare away demons, appease the gods, thank the spirits of animals before a hunt, attract rain, as integral elements of religious ceremonies, and to induce states of wonder and thanksgiving.

To quote Johnathan Fields in from his blog "Thinking on Music", August 29, 2014, "Theologians often treat music as a potent tool for fostering sacred awareness. Music's ethereal abstractness suggests a reality that is beyond the ability of words to describe. Of the resources available to humanity, musical sounds are the closest representation of the Divine. To quote Joseph Addison, they are 'all of heav'n we have below.' Yet, theologians are quick to remind us that music and theology are not the same. The absorbing impact and amorphous beyondness of music might hint at God's immanence and transcendence, but this effect is, at best, a useful metaphor."

I like to think of Sacred Music as more than a metaphor, but potentially a series of sounds that can go right to the heart of my Spirit and create an experience of elevated consciousness. Not unlike mantras, Sacred Music has a vibration to it that can induce a similar vibration in the listener. Steven Halpern, and many other musicians throughout musical history, has intentionally used music to create a particular response in the listener. Steven's career has centered on creating healing music that has vibrations to elicit certain responses in the body that are helpful to health and well-being.

To quote Steven's website, "Sound Healing is an umbrella term that focuses on the intentional use of sound and music to support the natural healing energies of the 'human instrument'. Sources of sound healing include instruments, voice, metal and quartz crystal bowls, tuning forks, drums and computer-based frequency generators."

Relaxation and the reduction of stress have been proven to be a fundamental building block to health, healing, well-being, and a healthy lifestyle in general (see The Relaxation Response by Herbert Benson MD). I've listened to Halpern's Spectrum Suite for a number of years as background and relaxation music and am also aware that it has healing properties to stimulate healing.

Some of his music speaks to different energy centers or "chakras" in the body and can activate healing in these centers.

I like to have Sacred Music playing in the background when I am working, relaxing, or while Lynne and I spend time in the evening "reasoning" together. We often have had the music system Pandora on and have set up several "stations" --James Taylor, John Denver, Bob Marley, the Guyoto Monks and Deva Premal. We listen to the Deva Premal the most, and based on our "likes", "dislikes" and Pandora's algorithm, have found the song, a chant, a mantra, Om Namah Shivaya, a Hindu song or bhajan coming up rather frequently. It's a tune that's been running through my brain for the past several days, including when I wake up at night. Have to say this is better than some "My Baby Done Me Wrong" song, or something more discordant, as the vibration that it sets up in my consciousness is much higher.

(I particularly like the version and the whole album Dakshina, from Deva Premal):

> Om Namah Shivaya Gurave, *(Om. Salutations to the guru, who is Shiva.)*
> Satchidananda Murtaye, *(His form is being, consciousness, and bliss.)*
> Nishprapanchaya Shantaya *(He is transcendent, calm,)*
> Niralambaya Tejase. *(Free from all support, and luminous.)*

I also like *Wikipedia's* explanation of this mantra:

> Traditionally, it is accepted to be a powerful healing mantra beneficial for all physical and mental ailments.

Soulful recitation of this mantra brings peace to the heart and joy to the [Atman] or Soul. Sages consider that the recitation of these syllables is sound therapy for the body and nectar for the Soul [Atman]. The nature of the mantra is the calling upon the higher self; it is the calling upon Shiva, the (Hindu) destroyer deity, to aid in the death (destruction of ego) and rebirth achieved during meditation. This goes generally for mantras and chants to different gods, which are different aspects of the higher self.

My takeaways from this:

- This chant is to that part of the Self that destroys and creates in meditation—destroys or transcends the body/mind/personality so that our point of attention can be on the Self, our Higher Consciousness.

- I don't know about you, but I'm one of those who has a song running through my brain from time to time, sometimes a silly, undesirable song. I have learned to substitute Om Namah Shivaya or Amazing Grace, for example, when another, undesirable song is "playing" in my brain. This conscious attunement of my point of attention is something that I find has become more and more important in recent times. Not just in not letting my mind and thoughts go where they will, willy nilly, but in taking control and sending my awareness where I want it to go. Om Namaha Shivaya is healthier for me than Wrecking Ball.

<u>Om Namah Shivaya</u> dissolves the body/mind/ personality's "song" and substitutes one that is about consciousness, bliss, transcendence. Its very vibration is therapy for the body and sweet acknowledgement for the Soul. Also, the rhythm of it is great for running. It makes that steep hill Sasha dog and I encounter twice daily easier to climb.

Here's some other music that I like that has the same effect:
- Beethoven's Ninth Symphony (all of Beethoven's symphonies, really)
- Bob Marley's "One Love"
- John Lennon's "Imagine"
- Cat Steven's "Morning has Broken"

Audio Tapes

Another way to tap into Higher Consciousness is the take advantage of audio and video recordings of books being read, talks being given, and idea snippets being presented on YouTube--free and low-cost downloads from YouTube, Amazon, Apple I Tunes, and other online sites. The amount and quality of information available is amazing. I have a few things that I am inclined to listen to over and over because they put me in a peaceful state of mind or inspire my imagination.

Here are some observations and then some resources:
- Listen to an inspirational audio recording--in the morning while you brush your teeth, while you are doing yoga, when going for a run, on the way to work, in the middle of the night when you wake up worrying about something. I have found this a particularly helpful

trigger for putting myself into a meditative or mindful state.

About two years ago I began listening to inspirational audio recordings frequently. This was an exceedingly difficult and stressful period, and I awoke many times in the middle of the night afraid for my job, worried for my future, thinking about how I was going to "survive".

I had been studying Joel Goldsmith (one of the twentieth century's greatest mystics) for years--his books and CDs obtained from his family's website: joelgoldsmith.com. Then I found a website (joelsgems.com) which had talks that I could download to my phone. I downloaded 6 or 7 of them and played them when I awoke and couldn't go back to sleep as my mind ran away from me in the darkness. I would plug in the earbuds and listen for hours sometimes. I also like listening to the <u>Eternal Om</u> 60-minute continuous loop tape from Dick Sutphin.

I didn't want to become too dependent on the tapes and use them as a crutch or get to where I can't go back to sleep without them but decided during this time of turmoil that a peaceful night's sleep, training my mind and dipping into Spirit while sleeping, was a desirable pursuit.

- As I wrote in my meditation journal before a legal hearing about the whistle blowing incident I mentioned in the first chapter: "It's helpful at night, when I awaken at 3:00 to go pee and can't go back to sleep quickly because my mind is spinning on about my hearing coming up and the questions I might be asked, to put on a meditation tape. I have several which last for 60 minutes and I usually go back to sleep with one of them on, short circuiting my reactive mind. I tell myself, 'I'll think about that in the morning' or 'I'll let my subconscious mind work on that'. This usually does short circuit my train of thought, replacing it with a different vein of thinking, and calms the pumping along of negative thoughts. In addition, I'm putting light into my subconscious mind, which is helpful any time, awake or not."

- It's the turning Within that helps; helps shift a thought stream from one track to a different, more conscious one. One that creates less karma, by substituting the undesirable track for one that uplifts, creates a higher vibration, and is more peaceful. Amazing how just taking a moment and saying "Peace, be still", or "Spirit is on the field here" can help me transcend the thoughts that take me down a rabbit hole. Sometimes listening to a tape recording for a few minutes is all I need to rise up into Higher Awareness. Then I can go on, renewed.

I am constantly doing mind training, training my mind to turn off and let Spirit come forward in its place; persuading my mind to slowly, slowly let go of the reins while engaging the world and its issues. Unlike some Zen stories of complete flashes of transformation from unconsciousness to sustained consciousness, my process is a slow, steady progression.

I guess by now you can tell that growing in consciousness is one of my passions and that I put quite a bit of attention on it--all of these methods I am offering are among my routines.

Books, Reading

Our bookshelves are filled with spiritual books we have collected and read on a variety of subjects. Their ideas have been inspiring and helpful to my spiritual growth. Often one or another "jumped" off the bookshelf at the bookstore, although these days we mostly buy them from the Amazon bookstore.

- I haven't done as much reading in the past couple of years since I began writing with the purpose of publishing. I haven't wanted to influence my writings with the ideas of others and consciously or subconsciously "borrow" somebody else's material. However, these writings are filled with ideas I have been exposed to over the years and incorporated into my understanding of the world, myself, and meditation.
- The reading I have done recently is mostly in the area of research on certain topics that I have been inspired to write about, something that I haven't done before in a systematic way.
- I like having my favorite books around and leave them purposely scattered about so that they are there at any moment I want to be inspired by them. I tend to turn down the pages so that favorite passages are easily accessible.

Moving Meditations

I am a very physical person and like to move my body in a number of different ways, including some that have elements of meditation and mindfulness built into them. The beauty of moving meditations is that they are generally done with the eyes open. It is challenging to the mind and body to accomplish a meditative state while in motion and can be practiced for a lifetime.

Here are some of my favorites.

Yoga. Yoga, for me, is such a wonderful way to stay loose--physically, mentally, emotionally, and spiritually. I began doing yoga over 45 years ago. It has a "stretching exercise" component to it and a sitting meditation component. I think yoga is best begun by taking a class. I particularly like Integral Yoga Institute system, but there are dozens of types of yoga available today from Iyengar, which has a strong healing component to it, to Bikram, that is done in a hot environment and is more like a gym workout. IYI has yoga centers all over the country or you can buy their Beginner Yoga CD series.

My advice: Do yoga. In the morning. First thing. If only for 10-15 minutes. Then a 4-10-minute HCM. I know, I know, regular yoga class takes 60-90 minutes. But after you've done it for a while you can pare it down to 6-8 poses that you like best. I especially enjoy the Salutation to the Sun. Yoga has the potential to help us increase our vibration as we learn to breathe, meditate, and move more consciously—all at the same time.

- **Tai Chi**. Tai Chi is my most recent moving meditation practice. Both Lynne and I went once or twice a week to a class at our local fitness center for a year. Like yoga it is a moving meditation. It also throws in balance and moving across the floor slowly and gracefully. It's practiced by millions in countries all over the world. We're taking a class with a great teacher, Peter Paul. Emphasizing the moves, in sequence, with proper technique, and being aware of the breath is part of the routine. The short version takes about 5 minutes, the longest about 14. The one I like the best, and still do twice a week at home, is the Competition Style, which takes about 9 minutes. I also bought a CD from Terry Dunn, Tai Chi for Health from which I have learned much about proper technique and is a way to get started if classes are not available to you in your area.

When Tai Chi is introduced into senior centers, falls and broken bones have been dramatically reduced. Our class of mostly people over 50 has become remarkably close and friendships have blossomed. It has given me a new set of learnings, realizations, and fun.

Through Tai Chi I am learning how to get more deeply into the "Zone", which is said to promote peak athletic performance. Being able to get into the Zone is what enabled elite athletes like basketball great Michael Jordan, football wiz Joe Montana and tennis legend, Arthur Ashe (who meditated on court during tennis matches), to perform at their peak when the pressure was on and the game was on the line.

- **Tennis**. I am applying the concept of meditation and the Zone to my tennis. It can be applied to any sport where focus and physical activity without a lot of mental effort is desirable. In tennis, to watch the ball coming toward you, and notice the spin and the bounce can be helpful in "letting the body hit the ball" as author Tim Gallwey put it in The Inner Game of Tennis. From time to time I am able to get into the Zone, a transcendent experience, and play significantly better than usual. The trick is to be able to get into the Zone at will. I'm still working on that and my ability to be aware of my breath before I serve is getting better.

There is also a great book called The Legend of *Bagger Vance*: A Novel of Golf and the Game of Life by Steven Pressfield on this same subject of getting into Zone. He calls the Zone "the Field" and has detailed instructions on its application to golf. These are principals you may to apply to your favorites sport. Another good book on the subject is The *Zen* of *Tennis*: A Winning Way of Life by Nancy Koran.

Here's how I described one experience with Zen Tennis in my meditation journal.

"Played tennis this morning with Mike, my usual tennis partner (when we lived in San Diego). He and I have been pushing each other to get better and it's getting to the point that to win a point I have to hit a winner; I can't just hope he will make a mistake. I did a nice meditation this morning and found myself "in the Zone" on the court, bringing Higher Consciousness to my experience of the match.

I was able see the ball better, hit it more cleanly and enjoy more deeply the give and take of the interaction with him. Played great, as did he, and I'm as pleased to see him hit a fabulous shot as I am to do that myself. There was a moment when I hit a particularly good shot that I thought, 'Take me now Lord, I'm ready to go on to Heaven'. He does a little mantra repetition to get himself centered, as well, which he learned from a girlfriend. Interesting, because he doesn't seem to be the type to do such a thing. Not mine to judge.

I breathe and allow myself to go within for "the feeling". It's so satisfying. Especially comparing my state of mind today to Thursday's when we played. That day I felt out of sync and wasn't "seeing" the ball. Consequently. I was spraying the ball everywhere, unsure of myself and my game.

I haven't found the key yet that unlocks the door yet to an, as they say, 'unconscious' (unbelievable playing without thinking about it) day on the court but am enjoying, even when I don't play particularly well, working with myself to bring consciousness into it. This supports my daily goal of being conscious, mindful, and to bring that into every activity possible. All "grist for the mill" as Ram Dass famously said in his book of the same name

It's through tai chi and tennis I have learned that Higher Consciousness is a learnable skill. It is a lifelong endeavor, of course, but not just a matter of a stroke of blessing from the angels. I suppose it's not a stretch to say that the pursuit of Higher Consciousness has become a lifestyle for me. The more I do this type of inner work the better I get at it (bringing consciousness into the moment); and the better I get at my physical activity and performance."

- **Walking (and running).** Lynne and I went for a retreat to Spirit Rock some months ago and found the walking meditation particularly intriguing. The instructions from Anna Douglas, the workshop leader, were to go out and walk the grounds, silently and with mindfulness.

"Start out by being aware of your body moving. Your feet taking you step by step down the path. Be aware of the movement of the feet in your shoes. Notice what part of the foot contacts the ground first and last. Listen to the noise of the gravel with each step. Begin to be aware of the noises around you. The birds and other animal life. The grass and the sun sparkling off it. The leaves of the trees and their rustle. The trees themselves. See if some don't have an aura you can pick up on. Feel the sun on your face. The breeze ruffling your hair. Do this for 20 minutes and we will ring a bell to call you in."

It was during one of these walks (we did several over the period of a day) that I had a realization that I shared with the group, "My Buddha Mind was taking my body for a walk, much like my taking my dog for a walk" and that "That my Buddha Mind was not going to die, in my experience, even though my body surely would." This was not a view, however, shared by all. Not surprising since the Buddha also admonished his followers not to believe everything, but they should take responsibility for trying out his ideas in their own experience.

The exercise instructions included the suggestion to "tune into each of your senses while you walk and see which of them you are particularly partial to". I found that I was most aware of the cacophony of the birds communicating with the rest of their immediate world to hear and share in their aliveness. The exercise brought me very much into the Now and the immediacy of the warmth of the sun on my face.

Since Sasha Dog takes me for a 1/2 mile run twice a day, I have begun to apply this mindful approach to my running, as well. I am almost always aware of the tightness in my muscles as I begin each jaunt through the neighborhood. I frequently concentrate on my breath, the inflow and the outflow; the difference in frequency when I am going uphill and down. I'm using my chiropractor Philip Runco's suggestion to inhale through the nose and exhale through the mouth. This gets maximum air into the lungs and maximum exhale. Very efficient.

I frequently use the Sacred Breath technique, mentioned earlier, when running in my neighborhood--breathing in Spirit on the inhale and radiating light out into the neighborhood on the outbreath; spreading goodwill. This and picking up trash along the way from time to time, saying hello to those I encounter are all a part of being a good neighbor, I suppose.

Sacred Scribbling

Even if you are not a writer, I suggest that you keep a journal of your journey into Higher Consciousness. Take a moment every day to note your thoughts and experiences about your meditation/mindfulness practice; even if you didn't meditate at all one day or even think about being mindful about anything. This is a real opportunity to capture your experiences and is a great learning tool.

The series of books that I will be publishing started out as notes about the unfolding and unfolding and unfolding of my life during the difficult time in San Diego that I mentioned earlier. Before long it was not only a chronicle of my daily learning and growing but also a way to capture and conceptualize what I was doing. It became my way to express from my Soul what was going on with me—the good, the bad, the ugly and the transcendent. It was very cathartic and therapeutic.

Write for yourself. Write for fun. Write to give yourself a record of significant and not so significant moments. It is a kick to go back from time to time to see where you have been as well as how much and how little progress you are making--especially the former. The latter will take care of itself. Sometimes what comes flowing through my fingers as I type amazes me, and I become cognizant of my HiC being my companion and teacher, offering encouragement and insight.

I find myself throughout the day being inspired to write something that flashes into my consciousness. Often it is a word or a phrase that comes full blown. I write the word or phrase down, and then go back and flesh out idea that I want to address.

I'll note the word or phrase down, sometimes on a 3 x 5 card, and pick it up later on in the day to write about it. Sometimes the words come in torrents, sometimes in bursts, sometimes just flowing, sometimes in dribbles. I try to capture as much of the feeling and nature of the words as I can to get at the essence of the insight that I had in that moment of a "flash".

I often sit in the evening after Lynne goes to bed and pick up on the theme from earlier in the day. Sometimes I "free write": sit, be quiet, and write down whatever comes. Here's how I described it one evening:

"The brow intensifies, the eyes narrow. Attention goes Within and becomes the Center while I peer out. Breath is more obvious and time collapses, collapses to Now as the only moment there is. This moment. These movements. A sense, at the edge of my awareness, of HiC observing and participating. In me. Through me. As me.

I type waiting for the next word and the next and the next. Flowing out. Pausing. Flowing out. My words or His? Yes. I can't say, actually, as attempting to do so breaks the mood. There it is again. The flow. Where does it come from, where does it go? Doesn't matter really as the flow in the moment is the thing that delights. Confuses. Clarifies.

Deep breath. Pause. Scratch my head, and it starts up again. The flow. It's fun to play with, to experiment with. To see where it goes even if it doesn't seem to be going anywhere in particular. A glow. A smile at the irony of letting go when my ego/mind says "No, don't. You're venturing out too far. Who knows where you'll go with this? Can't be good." And so it is, whatever it is. I choose to trust the process. Letting the writing write itself feels right, even if I say sillily clever things. I can feel the kinks loosening up a bit."

Try this. I think you'll like it. At least some of you will. And I invite you to offer other members of our community your writings, as well. As mentioned earlier, I will have a journaling app available in the next few months to write and make notes from your cell phone. Stay tuned!

Decision Making

One of the hardest things to do sometimes is to make a good

decision about what to do about something important at a key time. Follow these steps:

- Sit quietly for a few minutes and use the HCM meditation process outlined earlier to get yourself into a calm state.
- Define the issue as best as you can. Answer these questions: What is the issue? What are the alternatives? What are the impacts of the alternatives on yourself and others? What feelings do you have related to the alternatives? What have you already tried? What about that worked and didn't work?
- Ask your Higher Consciousness, "What about this HiC? I'm interested in the best possible outcome for everybody involved. Please offer me your perspective."

- Listen. Listen over several sessions, over several days if it's a complex and/or key decision. Write down what you "get" in your HCM sessions.
- Decide. Move on. Often your options are multiple "good" options. Choose the one that strikes you as having the highest vibration, the best outcome for the greatest number of people, the choice your HiC pointed to.
- See how your decision works out. Change your decision if it becomes apparent you made the wrong one, for whatever reason. Correct any negative impact your decision has had on others, if possible.

Appreciate and Be Grateful

One of the practices that is suggested by some of the Law of Attraction gurus to attract more "stuff" and experiences into your life is the practice of taking time every day to be grateful for what you already have.

As author Melody Beattie puts it, "Gratitude unlocks the fullness of life. It turns what we have into enough, and more. It turns denial into acceptance, chaos to order, confusion to clarity. It can turn a meal into a feast, a house into a home, a stranger into a friend."

Here's the interesting question to ask: "Why is this?" Perhaps because being grateful is a state of mind indicating Higher Consciousness, an attitude that lies "above the line" that Ruth Minshull draws in her classic book Choose Your People. In the book, "below the line" on her Tone Scale denotes negative emotions on a spectrum from apathy at the bottom to antagonism and boredom in the middle. Above the "line" are higher states of mind--contentment, mild interest, cheerfulness, and the like.

The more elevated one's consciousness the higher the vibration or tone on the scale. Gratitude, while not specifically mentioned, is exceedingly high on the Tone Scale. Gratitude indicates a level of development corresponding to an ability to "see", to "feel" into the 5th Dimension, which then "unlocks the fullness of Life" Ms. Beattie speaks of--Life Everlasting.

Gratitude is an attribute of an Illumined Mind. And that's the goal, an Illumined Mind. Gratitude is especially helpful in elevating our vibrations. It's hard to be grateful for something and be grumpy about it at the same time. A simple, heartfelt "thank you" can illumine a moment.

About this I wrote in my journal, "Gratitude is an attribute of Higher Consciousness, not Higher Consciousness itself, but an attribute--like love, joy, and peace that results from an Illumined Mind. The goal is Illumined Mind, Illumined Vibration. Resting in Eternity. Aware of Allness. Tickled by Knowing. Grateful to HiC for Its having revealed Itself in the isolation, nay, desolation, of 3d consciousness. Where we are mired in ignorance. 'Thank you for having saved me from the hell of ignorance, isolation, and foolishness, oh my Soul' "

My HiC says in return (this is the type of conversations we have), "You have achieved conscious realization and will never go back". To which I say, "Thank you". He says, "You are one with Spirit and know it". To which I say, "Thank you. 'Preciate it". Out of that knowing and trust flows the thought, "Spirit, into your hands I commit my being". Here's the pome (I'm not a poet, so I can't call it a poem) that flowed out:

Appreciate Appreciating

Appreciate. Appreciate. Appreciate appreciating.
Air to breathe. Life to live. Hot chocolate to quaff.
Wife to cuddle.
Taking the dog for her jaunt through the neighborhood,
Through the gauntlet of her buddies just straining to get out and play.
Cat purrrrr rrrrr rrrrr in the middle of the night.
Stuff that has agreed to surround me and protect me from the unknown Universe out there.
Atoms, cells, and electrons. My buddies.
At an agreed upon set of coordinates, every day, in the vastness of eternity.
Four wheeled steed, ready anytime I want to run off into the familiarly
unfamiliar, with all of the other steeds.
Jostling for space on the asphalt trail to my "Oh so important" destination, And back.
Safe in my cave. Again.

Appreciate the moon through the skylight,
Lighting up the drops of moisture diamonds.
Wind. Whipping down the leaves.
Rain splash, splash, splashing, dripping--sky's drum beat.
New, green grass, up through the cracks,
Aching to live. In my sidewalk.
Of all places to want to live. In my sidewalk.

Finding a little spot. To exist. To grow. To evolve.
Maybe to replicate the DNA and spawn a friend,
Companion in the vastness of who knows what.
Love you.

"There will be a day when one of us will be left alone",
Lynne says to me,
Not knowing what the hell we're talking about.
In this moment all is well.

One More Entry from My Journal--"Thank You Supply Chain"

As I sat outside this evening taking in the end of the day and having crackers and cheese and wine, a feeling of overwhelming gratitude came over me for the all of the elements of the supply chain that put these things before me—the people, animals, machinery, resources and all the rest that were part of the step by step process that caused me to relish a bit of Swiss cheese on a Triscuit cracker, washed down by a nice Napa Valley Chardonnay.

Tears came to my eyes for the time, effort, care and attention of the forces of the Universe that coalesced to nourish my body and mind, and ultimately my Spirit, as I sat there in a pool of intense thanksgiving for the moment. These nourishing things that I exchanged for pieces of paper or electrons; that manifested in my presence through the unfolding of events and circumstances. What a fortunate guy am I!

As I revisit that moment I am moved again at my good fortune.

Create a Higher Vibration in Your Home

Your home, your cave-- best place to work on upping the vibration around you. My observations:

- It has taken a while, but I am finally able to articulate what Lynne has done in each of the homes we have lived in together—create an elevated vibration and continue to work on that vibration day by day, week by week, year by year. She does this by:
  - o Using her visualization abilities to "see" better arrangements of furniture, colors, textures, holiday and festive themes, food, and other smells,
    arrangements of all things outside, and more.
  - o Using me to do what I do best. I'm the mover, the handyman, the hanger of pictures and mirrors, the hole digger.

- I've come to realize how important this is. A home has a vibration based on many things including location, design, use of materials, as well as the mental, emotional, physical, and spiritual state of mind of the people and other animals living there.

- I've also come to realize that an individual or a group/family can intentionally increase the vibration in some of the ways mentioned above and others including, you will be surprised to hear me say this, the contemplative practices of the people living there.

- Creating a favorable vibration is one of the key elements of the Chinese practice of Feng Shui (see below).

- Higher vibration contributes to the well-being of the people living there if done with consciousness and intention. One of the key messages in my writing is the notion that by increasing the rate of your vibration you increase your state of your awareness, with profound implications in every area of your life.

- A higher rate of vibration can be achieved in any environment, no matter how high or low a rate of vibration you start with. Using meditation and creativity you can turn something good, bad, or indifferent into something better.

- Start from wherever you are.

You might also find it helpful to use some of the following tools we have encountered to increase the vibration of our home. For example, we have a friend, Maria Carter, who is a Feng Shui coach. Feng Shui is a Chinese practice of being aware of and channeling the energy (called chi) in and around your dwelling to optimize your quality of life.

Maria visited our home in San Diego, made extensive notes, and developed a floor plan of the layout of the house. Based on her observations, and consulting with the Feng Shui system of arranging furniture, along with using color, plant life, fountains, and various other "remedies" to strengthen "weak" areas of the house, she developed a set of suggestions about the things that we might address to improve our lives.

During her visit she interviewed us and asked us interesting questions about what we wanted in relationship to certain areas of our lives that Feng Shui addresses: money, career, friendship, etc. These life "areas" correspond with the 9 areas of the house that Feng Shui examines, resulting in 9 statements of intention which we recorded, put in envelopes, and scattered about the house in strategic out-of-sight places.

One of the remedies she offered, for example, was to address a weakness in the "wealth" corner of our house, which happened to be our master bedroom, and change the colors of our curtains and bedspread, as well as place indoor plants on a silver tray in the room to enhance our financial wellbeing.

Using her suggestions and our own interpretation of her suggestions, we made a number of changes around the house that resulted in a subtle, but improved, heightened vibration in the house. The theory is that by making your home more "conscious" and using a system that has a coherent structure to it, it is possible to attract more of what you want, and less of what you don't want. I will address the issue of the Law of Attraction more in a later book.

Pray over the News

I watch the national news most nights because I'm interested in the day's events and want to know some of what is going on with this human tribe to which I belong. It gives me insight into the human condition---a daily journal of our collective psyche. In January 2019 as I write this, the focus in the United States is mostly on the craziness is going on here in the Trump era.

Typically, the focus of the news is on the bad, the ugly, and the foolish. (NBC news, thankfully, has begun to end each broadcast with a story about somebody or some people who are making a positive contribution.) Before the news comes on, I do a 30 second to 2-minute meditation in which I go into my Within-ness and contact my HiC. As each story unfolds, staying in that state of Withiness, I let Spirit flow into the story, especially those that are sad, outrageous, and which display gross ignorance.

By putting myself in a state of Higher Consciousness and "seeing" what's going on from a more enlightened point of view, I am able to allow Spirit to move through me to do what It will to alleviate suffering, to elevate unconsciousness. I attempt to see the Higher Consciousness of the "goobers" I see through this "window" into the human condition on Earth in the early part of the 21st Century.

Sometimes it's hard to see past the surface horror of what we do to each other, day by day, one atrocity after another; each fading before resolution is reached for the next creative craziness we come up with. Yet, a higher state of awareness enables me to observe, sacredly, and to see humanity growing, however haltingly, in its evolution.

I asked HiC one evening, "What's going on here?", referring to several news stories that were highlighted. Here's what He said,

- *In Iraq and across the Middle East, the ISIS militants are ablaze in their fervor, drunk with their cruelty. Even Al Qaeda is appalled. This is perhaps the beginning of the end of tribalism.*

> • *As for Robin Williams, he was a sacrificial lamb to celebrity; a tender heart. His ego/mind could not deal with his depressed view of the world anymore. He is now in a much better place.*

I'm convinced that this "praying" contributes to the evolution of our collective consciousness and lifts it up ever so slightly. I also think that by letting Spirit flow into the various events, that a bit of healing occurs. Since I usually watch a recording of the news, I am able to skip the commercials and those stories that I don't feel much affinity towards: weather difficulties and the like.

Daily Life Situations. Go Within to Your Inner Sanctum

Every day, as I move through my day, there are situations that come up that are annoying, maddening, frustrating, and stupid. For example, as I wrote in my journal on November 22, 2013, "Today my former landlord sent me a letter telling me that not only was he not refunding any of my deposit of $2100, but that I owed him an additional $300 for all the work that it took to turn the clean house that we had left him, in nearly spotless condition.

This is annoying, maddening, frustrating, and stupid. I could easily get upset, pissed off, and call him a jackass. However, I was able to stop, take a few deep breaths, go Within, find that place where HiC resides, and radiate light to the situation and to the landlord. I also (I wrote) must do research into what my rights are and follow up appropriately."

This I did. I found that he had violated California landlord law. I sent him a letter detailing the statute and his violations, indicated that I would take him to small claims court if necessary, and received a full refund the next week. The turning point was pausing and going Within for my answer.

Questions to Consider

Which ones of these "Other Ways of Tapping into Higher Consciousness" appealed to you? Why?

Make a list of two or three of these that particularly seem appealing. Explore one of them for a few days, a week, and see where it takes you. What happened?

Do any seem particularly obnoxious? What bothers you about it/them?

CHAPTER 9

Triggers, Tips and Other Reminders

As I have become more conscious, I find I want to become yet more and more aware; to meditate more, to see from my Higher Consciousness more, to raise my vibration more. Remembering to remember to be awake has become a passion. I want to be in that Place more and more often. But my body/mind/personality doesn't always fully cooperate. It sometimes wants to be in control and to keep me hypnotized. It's lazy and resistant, this 3d consciousness of mine.

Six minutes, and longer, Higher Consciousness Meditation sessions are a fundamental ingredient to the development of my Awareness, but I have found that they are not enough. As a result, I have dug into my understanding of adult learning techniques and developed a set of triggers to help me remember. Most of them are intended to couple a kinetic, physical activity with an intended spiritual outcome, and work pretty well.

The creation and use of these triggers are based on longing. Every time I come back to my Withiness I feel like I have been absent from a friend. I think "Ah, too bad, I like this Place". I miss it and think I "should" spend more time there. These short, frequent mini-meditations, or mindfulness exercises that follow, will raise your consciousness if only for a few moments. The benefits are cumulative, however, and will contribute to your overall growth in Awareness.

It has been my experience that making the transition from a less aware life to a more aware life is a process that takes time and is a continuous learning experience. It's rather like the transition a baby makes from crawling to walking. My little grandson was 9 months old, when I wrote this. He began crawling about 6 weeks ago after a month of rolling over onto his stomach, getting up on his hands and knees, rocking back and forth and then taking his first crawl step. He went through the process of standing up and bouncing, with help, stretching his feet out from curled to flat, pulling himself up to a standing position, and taking a few steps with the help of his fire truck.

Walking is a difficult process for all infants and his learning to walk and run will involve many more fits and starts with many falls and scraped knees. Learning to get up from our 3d reality and "walk" into 5-Dimensional Reality is a similar learning experience. Fits and starts, fits and starts, but with an upward trajectory toward Higher Consciousness.

Each of his steps along the way is a developmental stage and he is getting a lot of support from the world about him on his journey to running a 100-yard dash. The triggers I offer in this chapter are tools and tricks to train our body/mind/personality to let go and let our Spirit/Mind to be our predominant focus of attention.

Triggers can put us directly into a state of Higher Consciousness (I hope you are beginning to see that Higher Consciousness is nothing mysterious. It's available at any moment we turn to it, and triggers are great ways to do that.) Try them. Day to day, moment to moment, these additional techniques can be used almost anytime, anywhere, under any circumstance, without bothering others but greatly benefitting us. Each time we touch in with a trigger our vibration takes jump; we "vibe up" at least for a moment. Over time these jumps contribute to permanent, small, incremental changes.

Browse through these offerings and make notes of a few you want to try, right away. Others you may want to save for later. Some won't suit you at all. In any case, you won't be able to do them all at the same time. That would be too much, too soon—information overload. Experiment. Find out what works for you. Keep in mind that something that seems helpful today may fade in its efficacy over time—you may successfully incorporate the learning and need something new. One approach may get boring and need to be replaced with another.

There is a variety here to keep you busy. I will also explore them more thoroughly in the companion to this book <u>Six Second Mindfulness Meditations</u>. Many of you, however, will become creative and develop your own techniques to remind yourself to remember to stay Awake.

Mantras--Sacred Words and Phrases

"Mantra" is a "Sanskrit word which refers to a sacred utterance, sound, syllable, word, or group of words believed by some to have psychological and spiritual power," according to Wikipedia. A mantra itself may or may not have a literal meaning; the spiritual value comes when it is heard, uttered or present in thought.

Furthermore, according to Wikipedia, "The earliest mantras were composed in Vedic times by Hindus in India and are at least 3000 years old. Mantras are now found in various schools of Hinduism, Buddhism, Jainism and Sikhism. Similar hymns, chants, compositions and concepts are found in Zoroastrianism, Taoism, Christianity and elsewhere." Almost every religion, really.

I like to think of a mantra as a word or phrase that elevates our Awareness when said once or over and over with sacred intent. Mantras are used to go Within for a sacred moment, to shift our awareness from 3d to 5D consciousness, and raise our vibrations. Without intent they are useless to us as spiritual tools. With intent they can be powerful learning and remembering tools.

The Transcendental Meditation community, in their indoctrination process with folks new to their practice, give a mantra which is said to be perfectly suited to that person to each new TM meditation student. **Eng, em, shirim, hirim, kirim, kiring, sham and shama** are said to be some of those used and are to be repeated over and over in their meditation process.

"Spirit and I are One. My life emanates from this". This is my personal core principal. This is a phrase I use at least once a day when I can take a moment and feel the vibration of it. It is similar to Jesus of Nazareth's **"I and my Father are One"**. It works better for me because it puts Spirit first, not "I" and uses the term "Spirit" rather than "Father". "Father", in today's vernacular, is too much like the old man with a beard sitting on a throne, rather than "Spirit", the underlying principal of the Universe that is Omnipresent. This Spirit radiates from my Being out into my world.

I particularly like to use the phrase "**Peace, be still**", used by Jesus, it is said, to quieten the storm in which he and his followers found themselves out on the Sea of Galilee. This is a phrase that we can use to calm the storm, large or small, that might be occurring in our minds or right in front of us. Saying this can immediately put us in a different state of mind, a Higher Consciousness state of mind that can make it easier for us to cope with whatever situation we find ourselves in. Or it can just be used to increase our vibration and put us in a calmer, more desirable state of mind, shifting our interior state and point of view.

Another one of my favorites is "**Go Within, stay Within**". As I wrote in my meditation journal about this one:

"In today's meditation I came to realize how responsible I am for my own peace of mind/state of mind. My body/mind/ personality can take me into all sorts of directions and emotional states to keep me entertained and committed to its way of operating and living life. Up and down. Up and down. Sideways.

The Spirit/Mind way is elevated consciousness and heightened awareness. The choice is mine. I can drift with the body/mind/personality current or allow Spirit/HiC to raise my vibration by paying attention to it. This has to be a conscious choice, over and over. Moment by moment. Hour by hour. Turning Within, turning Within.

The reward of the latter is immense. A peaceful state of mind, a feeling of lightness and space, an anticipation of, the movement of Spirit. This sounds easy but it is not, in my experience. The easier thing is to go with the flow of 3d reality. The harder way is to remember and to allow Spirit to lead the way. The latter takes vigilance in where my attention is placed, Within or without. "Go Within, stay Within"; my mantra for the day."

Sacred words and phrases, then, can be used as trigger mechanisms any time you choose to shift your awareness. Used thusly, they can strengthen and enhance our meditation practice throughout the day, as reminders and vibration enhancers.

Some others that I like and use:
- **"I Am that I Am"** --which God was supposed to have said to Moses when he received the 10 Commandments. This one reminds me that Spirit, Allness, Is, and that I Am One with It. Something worth remembering, don't you think?
- **"Om"** --said to be the sound or vibration of the Universe, is nice to repeat. It is sung for an hour, over and over, on one my favorite recordings, "<u>Eternal Om</u>", by Dick Sutphin. I love listening to it in the middle of the night and while meditating.
- **"I am divine love"** --one Lynne likes a lot and which she used extensively when she was dis-eased with cancer and during cancer treatment. She still uses it today, years after becoming cancer free.
- Some others:
  - **I am divine joy**
  - **I am divine light**
  - **I am divine communication**

o **I am divine thought**
o **Creativity flows out**
o **Freedom from fear is mine**
o **I am One with Eternity.**
o **I am Eternity, Being**
o **I am an Eternal Being.**
o **"I will keep him in perfect peace whose mind is stayed on Me"**, Christian *Bible*
o **I live, move, and have my being in Spirit** (slight modification of "In Him I live, move and have my being".
o **"Be Present in The Presence in this Present Moment"** or simply **"Be Present"**. Here's what I wrote about this one:

"This is my mantra for the week, maybe my lifetime--to help me to remember to be present. To remember throughout the day my foremost purpose, growth in consciousness. This mantra helps me to get into a state of awareness or state of presence, state of mind-less-ness, so as to contact my Presence, my HiC, and to do so in the Now. At times I seemed to drop down into that state, to ground myself in It, and to drop out of a "thought run away" moment.

My senses heighten, locus of awareness shifts, and I smile. It's my happiest state, a sense of bubbling up of Spirit, which then spreads out like a light being slowly turned on in a room. Timelessness occurs. A Sacred Breath. Or a little piece of Truth comes floating in--Divine Judgment about what's going on.

It helps to have mantra like this from time to time as consciousness unfolds, as recognitions or realizations occur. Words come flowing to mind. Changing the mantra is also helpful. New sustenance comes, synapses fire off, "ahas" aha. A new mantra becomes the song to be sung in the moment, then becomes a bit stale as the learning is absorbed, and it becomes time to take on a new one--one that is appropriate for my next step.

One of the blessings of making contact with HiC is that it feeds the hunger for Spirit, for "the feelin", for contact with that elevated state, Heaven. He is my lifeline to Eternity, the crossover point that never gives up giving. This is when I feel most myself, when I have hit that sweet spot and, for the moment, am at peace. Sometimes it only lasts a moment; other times, a few moments. Sometimes for quite a while. I appreciate and cherish each episode. "

A more detailed list of mantras, their use, their meaning, and their efficacy is offered in the Six Second Mindfulness Meditations.

Other Quickie Mindfulness Meditations

I edited this book during the Covid19 Pandemic and know from talking to my daughter-in-law and others that being cooped up with your kids (and husband) 24 hours per day, 7 days per week, can by trying. Lovely as they are, kids tend to take all of the oxygen out of the room and can get on your nerves, big time.

Here are a couple of mindfulness exercises for the adult and the kids.

- For Mom and Dad:
  - Take a moment and "soften" your eyes. Then look at your child and "see" their Higher Consciousness Self. This make take a time or two to "click" in but the first time, in particular, can be a "Wowser". The child may notice that you have just looked at them differently and comment on the experience. In any case, you will never see her/him the same way again. Her Big Self, Soul, is much bigger than the body she occupies.

- For Mom or Dad and Child:
  - Suggest that your child take a deep breath and let it out slowly. She will probably take a quick, shallow breath. Then say "Let's do this together" and take a deep breath and let it out slowly. Again, she may do it quickly as you do it "better". And say "Let's try it again", modeling what you want. After a few times, though, she will get the idea and everything will settle down some. You and she.. I frequently do this with my two young grandsons when putting them to bed at night when they stay over at our house. Takes a bit to time, but they have gotten used to the idea and are go to sleep in 10 minutes or less after some wiggling and giggling.

- Write a word or phrase at the top of your notepad as you begin a meeting. I usually just write "I" or "I Am" and circle it (as in the "I Am that I Am" mantra, above).

This helps me to go Within when the meeting gets dull or heated or needs a moment of light.

- Use a small stone, or crystal, placed on or around your computer as a trigger. I had a white, round, smooth stone that I placed on my laptop as a kinetic reminder. I say "had" because Kitten Cleo stole it recently and I had to replace it with another stone, a polished quartz. I place it where I have to move it around from time to time and the act of doing so gives me a little "jolt" of spiritual energy since I have programmed myself to recognize it as such.

- Put sacred art items on your desk, on the wall where you often sit, and in the garden. I have little Buddha statues at the two places where I write the most (I like to move around from place to place when I write). I have pictures on the wall. We have statues of sacred figures in the garden and in various places in the kitchen. Not as objects of worship but as objects of reminder.

- Do one random act of kindness every day. Just for fun. Just to see what kind of reaction you get. Here your imagination can run wild for things to do, from opening a door for someone, leaving a dollar on the street, holding the elevator a moment longer, paying for someone's meal at the drive thru window, or letting someone into your traffic lane when you don't have to. There was a story on the news recently at Christmas time about a wealthy individual who used policemen to help him give away $100,000 in $100 bills to folks the officers came across who needed help. Most of the recipients wept with joy and relief.

- Be as happy to see your dog as she is to see you. See her divinity. In fact, be as happy to see your friend, significant other, child, or co-worker as your dog is to see you. See their divinity. It will brighten their day, for sure. But don't drool on them.

There are a lot more of these in Book 3 <u>Six Second Mindfulness Meditations</u>. Sign up below for our email list and I will let you know when it's available.

Have fun with these. Don't do them if it's a chore. Remember though-- they are just sooooo good for you! :)

Questions to Consider

What triggers have you used in the past, around this or any other subject? Describe your success. If you haven't used triggers what do you think about trying some?

Which ones would you like to start with? (Only choose a few) Why these? What outcomes would you like to have?

After a few weeks, come back and reflect on your experience. How did it go?

Have you developed any of your own? How did that go? What do you want to try next?

CHAPTER 10

Meditation Stories

I have sprinkled some meditation stories, and realizations that came out of them, throughout this book, but I thought I would also offer some at the end that don't quite fit into any other topic. I do this because of my own frustration with other authors and teachers on this subject. I would love to take a peek into the process of others on their journey, but this is not typically available. I don't know why; perhaps it's too personal. But I think that we can learn so much from each other, especially from key, unvarnished moments.

One weekend, for example, many years ago, I drove down to San Luis Obispo to hear Sri Swami Satchidananda speak. He gave a great talk in which, among other things, he said that being a householder was one of the hardest paths to enlightenment, much harder than living in a monastery or ashram. During the question and answer period I asked, "Would you tell us what it was like when you first began to experience enlightenment?" He gently deflected my question, which was disappointing.

Now, I know how hard it is to put such an experience in words. No words can really capture the experience of Illumination. But I didn't know that at the time. I'd hoped he would share a moment of personal experience.

These stories are re-writes of notes I made at the time they happened, at various times since I began doing Higher Consciousness Meditation in 2014.

In any case, my desire is to share my process, including my conversations with HiC. These accounts from my meditation journal may shed some light on the richness and power of the HCM process and may be helpful to you along your path. As you undertake your journey you may have similar experiences. Write them down. They are fun to review from time to time. I hope you enjoy them.

Breathe Me

There are times when "I" am no longer in the movement of atoms, cells and electrons of my body and become Spirit juice. These moments used to be fleeting and I would worry that I would lose the sense of Presence by thinking about it. These days, the Presence is right there every time I turn Within, ready to creep in, or to flood in, and leave me awash in the certainty of our merging together in the sacred marriage of the Ages.

One evening I said to HiC, "Breathe me. And fill me. Allow me the chance to be fully me without encumbrance" I breathed, in and the out. From a place of the deepest calm I've ever known. "I'm cradled in Divine Essence". Ideas flash. Concepts coalesce. Words gather to poorly represent the inflow of an experience I didn't expect to be given access to. Yet, here I am, being breathed by my Soul. Now-ing the Now. Unfolding the next moment and the next and the next.

I wrote, "I hate for it to go away. I hate to come to the realization that I have strayed from my point of attention in the Now to something in the future, or the past, or something wanted, or not wanted or many of the other distractions that I could be swept away by." "Just stay here", I say to myself, determined to savor the taste of Immortality.

And now I am breathing easier. The tightness has passed, and I am back in the "groove", into remembering to breathe. The Gratefulness exercise (that I did) helped. Saying "I am grateful for ..... (Fill in the blank)" is a good meditation exercise. It's good for acknowledging where I am. For allowing myself to chunk up in vibration and leave the lower vibration thoughts behind.

Majnoon

Irreverent and insightful Rabbi Winkler spoke of God in a radio interview I heard on an alternative San Francisco radio station this afternoon about an Arabic word "majnoon", which is both translated as "crazy" and "drunk with God". I thought, "That's how I feel sometimes, 'crazy' and 'drunk with God'".

Drunk with God. What a great term for being just immersed in Spirit to the point of being in an altered state of consciousness-- which is what it is. It's a great feeling, when, in a deep meditation, an altered state of consciousness occurs. Fifth Dimensional Consciousness. A weird place to find myself in compared to my Lutheran upbringing where <u>any</u> emotional response to a Sunday morning service was unusual except when my father belted out Martin Luther's famous hymn, "A Might Fortress is Our God".

Being high on God was not common where I grew up in North Carolina, except in black churches. Now that was different. The singing there could transport you to the gates of Heaven itself, the rocking and rolling that went on. I didn't know that I was experiencing "majnoon" the few times I went. But there you have it--proof that all religions are essentially the same when one is transported to 5D Consciousness by the experience. What follows is a "majnoon" experience.

This Morning

This morning I had another very powerful meditation. I felt like my vibration went through the roof as I sat on my yoga mat. The effect lasted much of the day and several times when I turned my attention in that direction, the intensity returned. Amazing.

When I asked HiC, He said, *"As much as you can handle, as quickly as you can handle it, is my approach with you. It always surrounds and is available to you"*. Gulp. I mean, "Yea". This is good news and makes it even more obvious that I am creating my own reality, including creating 5D experiences.

Makes sense. Given that 5D Reality surrounds and interpenetrates 3d reality, It is undoubtedly strong all of the time. My ability to perceive it is dependent on my ability to "see", to "feel", to "experience" the experience of being buoyed up by Spirit. "Drunk with God"; I like it.

"It's All Sacred"

This continues to surface as an "aha" insight. Sitting in the back yard this evening, with the full moon coming up over the hill, conversing with Lynne, cat purring on my lap, I had a strong feeling of the sacredness of my human experience. "It's All Sacred", flashed into my consciousness. Everything within my immediate vicinity glowed. Gives me shivers even now.

I was in and out of this state frequently for a few days, sometimes for longer periods, sometime shorter. Driving to our friends' house required my attention and the day had a lovely brightness, even in the overcast. Now, as I sit here reliving the experience, the feeling is typing the words as I try and capture it. Amazing Grace is all I can say about it. Off to bed with me. Thank you HiC…"*You're welcome good buddy.*" Can we do it again sometime? "*But of course. Welcome home.*"

Illumination

"Lumined, lit up, alight. All good descriptions of the higher realms I began to experience Higher Consciousness through Higher Consciousness Meditation. I'm beginning to touch this realm. Sometimes for sustained periods of time; 20 -30 minutes at a time. Other times just a flash, like now, as I write this", I wrote four years ago. Not something I would even have imagined five years previous to that. At that time, I had taken a new job as a leader of a team of consultants and manager of the region. I had a tiny apartment and went back and forth to my hometown, 60 miles away, because my wife and the house we had built on the river were there.

I was pretty comfortable and pretty cocky, as I had begun to turn the group around and we were headed in the direction of becoming a team and doing the right things to be successful. I was growing slowly but surely in my spiritual development, but my focus was on work. Don't know that I was meditating regularly, unless you consider doing yoga postures a meditation (which I do). And I was applying my awareness to trying, and often succeeding, at getting in "the zone" when playing tennis.

Much has happened since then, most notably a deep dive into Higher Consciousness, especially in the past two years--some of the more difficult in my professional career. Meaningful meditations have become a commonplace occurrence but feeling illumined is relatively new. This morning was one of those times. I had time to meditate for more than an hour and, at one point, I felt my vibration rise remarkably, aided by HiC (I'm convinced he is leading me step by step, into higher and broader realms).

My breathing took on a life of its own. It seemed as if Universal energy was flowing in and then radiating out into the Universe. Kind of a rhythmic two beat intake and then a longer outflow, with a pause at the end. I felt a bit lightheaded, more ephemeral really, and like I was being breathed by Eternity. Each exhale was a Universe inhale; likewise, with the inhales. My third eye area was activated and part of the billowing. I smiled and giggled. I put my tongue against the roof of my mouth--said to better connect the third eye with the lower part of the body and the heart through the chakra located in the throat.

My lips began trembling, involuntarily, as if something important was being said without any sound. This is a bit odd, I must, say but I decided to just go with it. I'm good hands with HiC and the feeling of being lifted up, swept up, into another realm was palpable—a lighter realm, a brighter realm, a realm with more freedom.

(This "communication" from HiC is more in the realm of gossamer stirrings of life/breath wings. Distinct thoughts seemed to bubble up every so often from a pool of life of which I am a part.) HiC suggested that I open my eyes and, shazam, everything seemed to take on a glow--furniture, dog Sasha, cat Annie, the floor. I closed my eyes and sensed that all was profoundly well with the Universe.

My right knee began to have a sensation and I stretched my legs out in front of me to give it, them, a bit of a stretch. The experience remained. The dog, thinking I might be getting ready to get up and take her for a run, got excited and came over to put her nose up against mine, giving me a lick. I laughed and resumed my cross-legged position, adjusting my meditation pillow.

The experience persisted. HiC seemed to turn up the vibration a notch. I could hear my heart beating in my head, a slight pounding. My breath became shallower, a slight in and out, in and out. I was a fascinated observer. It seemed that the 5th Dimension was flowing out through me into Eternity, bathing me in the process. Lynne got up, came through the room on the way to the bathroom. I held up my hand and she touched it lightly. I settled up again into my reverie.

I stretched my legs out again sometime later and began to put my running shoes on. Out in the street the feeling continued. I let Sasha pee and laughed at her glance of relief. We set off. The experience persisted. As I ran, I looked down at the street with squinting, fuzzy eyes, observing the slap slap of my feet and the woosh woosh of my breath. I looked up and the trees seemed alight in their distinct shape, color, and aura. HiC said, *"This is illumination. Enjoy it. It's yours anytime you want it. It's when you and I are the closest... to ... being...... One. It frees me up to roam and play in your world."*

Up the hill we went, breath coming more sharply. The big dog at the top of the hill gruffed, and gruffed and gruffed, lighting up the little yapper across the street. Sasha looked both ways to see if we were being attacked, but all was well. We reached the crest, and my leg burn reached its height of intensity. Swooping down the hill I felt the exhilaration of blood pounding in my ears. The grass rejoiced. I felt blessed.

Holy of Holies

For months I felt angry, frustrated, victimized, and wrathful about having been fired from a job, a profession that I loved so, and had developed a certain level of mastery of. I was extremely attached to it and to all it meant to me and about me. To a degree, I **was** my profession.

One evening, after Lynne went to bed, I had an amazing meditation in which I saw my part in all that occurred and that the time had come for me to leave for something else, which turned out to be my writing.

Afterwards I wrote, "Wow! It's hard to even describe the meditation that just occurred. In it I saw myself as a wounded warrior, out on a battlefield. Angels of mercy were combing through the bodies lying around, but few were still alive. One came over to me and saw that I was still breathing. She put her hands on me, mumbled something I didn't recognize, and suddenly I felt jolted by the energy that zapped me. She got up and began to walk away. "Wait", I said, "What just happened?" "Ask your HiC", she said and disappeared.

So, I did.

"Deep seated wounds are letting go. Body/mind/personality thoughts are fewer and are easier to be dissolved in the light of scrutiny. Your subconscious mind is being 'lightened' with Light. This is great because it's loosening the ties that bind you so tightly to the 'Wheel' of Birth and Death.

Daily, lower level 'stuff' will bounce off of you as you rise in Consciousness. Their vibrations will be too low to stick. Other lower level 'stuff' lies embedded in your personality, your ego/mind. Much will evaporate; some will float up to be released. None is too big to not 'leave the premises' unless your body/mind/personality is attracted to it in a way that becomes the dominant 'itch' to be 'scratched', causing you to go unconscious. This is only temporary, however, and will transmute as soon as you bring sufficient consciousness to bear. Hence, the value of meditation, communion with Spirit. It generates the elevation of Consciousness to vibrate away the 'stuff'. It is Spirit's gift to all individualized Consciousnesses.

A good way to proceed, at any time, is to say to the appearance of an internal or external 'glitch-- 'Peace, be Still' and then get still to let Spirit intervene. In time, maybe now. maybe later, the pressure/problem/gestalt will begin to lessen. Be so, so, so, careful though, that you have no expectation as to outcome; Spirit must be allowed to do what It will do for the best outcome within Allness. The impact may never be seen in your lifetime. It may be a correction of a past life or a future life occurrence. The impact may not occur in any way that you would be able attribute until you rise up in Consciousness where you can see with Spirit Eyes. Then all is perfect. Don't you find that interesting?"

To the reader: Of course, I do. And I have seen and felt effects that I would say were related to the movement of Spirit in a way that clearly transcended 3d reality. Something shifted "reality" in a way that it was clear that something "stirred". If the way I am describing this is disconcerting, annoying or "airy fairy" not to worry. Just spend some time here and let Spirit and your HiC go to work. It will become familiar one of these days. And you'll say, "Oh, that's what he meant. Why didn't he say so?" And I'll say, "I tried but the words failed me".

HiC went on to say, *"'Look' from this place, your Holy of Holies, and see if Eternity doesn't shift for you. At some point in your meditation there is a shift, usually a larger intake of breath, which indicates the threshold of your Holy of Holies is being crossed. There may be a going back and forth for a while until you settle in. Then magic occurs—and you are shown the true nature of 5D Reality. Internally, without form. You'll 'know' it when It happens—the light of Awareness turns on. Isness happens. As Paul Simon sang, 'I know what I know, I said what I said.' In this case, Oneness with the All."*

The further I go with my personal evolution into 5D Consciousness the more aware I am of the distance difference between the 3d and 5D "worlds". The more time I spend in Higher Consciousness Meditation the more aware I am of the increase in my vibration. In addition, I am aware that lower level vibrations, thought, feelings, and everyday events are dissolving before they occur or dissolving in the light of Consciousness.

Beholder

I am interested in personal enlightenment in this lifetime. How's that for a type A personality? It's not happening as fast as I would like. Perhaps because I am a householder and dealing with day to day issues of being out in the world rather than in a Zen center, focused on meditation and transformation 24/7. Don't know because I don't know that world and what its dynamics might be. In either case, the desire is internally induced. With me it is back and forth, between 3d consciousness and 5D Consciousness. When will the "flip" occur? Can't say. I can only address my experience, the only one I'm having, and my particular gestalt.

Joel Goldsmith suggests that one way to "get there" is to take the role of Beholder, to continuously step the body/mind/personality back and let Higher Consciousness "take over".

This seems risky, which is what a Grasshopper would say. Here is my dialogue with HiC about that.

"How am I going to get out of the way to be a Beholder of at You at work?", I ask HiC.

HiC reassures me, "*You are am doing fine and moving along nicely*".

"When, though, when will the flip occur? When will I become fully enlightened?"

"*When it does, of course, and not before. When 'Peace, be still' is you, not just something you say. When you have achieved a level of vibration in which you don't fall into your body/mind/personality's orbit any longer. When Higher Awareness ceases to come and go but remains steady, a light of continuous glow instead of a flickering of off and on. You will notice the change when your consciousness flickers like a fire. Always flickering-- brighter, not as bright, brighter, not as bright, brighter. A sudden, complete moment of Awakening is possible but happens to few. That is why this life can be frustrating, because you know where you want to be but aren't there yet.*

I know it's difficult to turn your life over to me, because you, seemingly, could go out of control. In fact, you're more in control than you ever have been, and 'Something' is guiding the process, a process that might be not evident for a while in its outcome. Impacts take a while to take shape, especially when the beginning of a change in consciousness is not that distant in the past. Especially if a calm spot is hit and you seem to be in limbo.

Not to worry. This is but a lull between states. It's hard to gauge where you are because the territory is new. Each person has his own schedule and reaction to the present "goings on". Trust is being developed, especially trust in the reality of a new dimension of consciousness. 3d is sooooooo ingrained. So deep in the psyche."

"So, you are saying, 'Patience, Grasshopper?' "

"You got it".

Fear

I woke up this morning with a hollow, full, fear ball in my belly. Perfect location, don't you think, in my third chakra? Didn't really attempt to go into the whys and wherefores of what this was about because it seemed so archetypical, somehow. I still am carrying around fear and it was so clear to me a symptom of my body/mind/personality's insanity.

I have nothing to fear, no real problems that are unmanageable. It was like I was tuned into the fear channel, the band of the emotional spectrum tuned into channel FEAR.

So, I sat right down, no preliminaries, and went right into my HCM Process. I began by breathing into it. The fear. Deep breaths. Belly breaths. Long and slow. After a little it began to break up—a bit. I began to say to myself, "Peace, be still" over and over. Over and over. This began to "loosen" it more.

Turning Within, I began to feel my vibration, ever so slowly begin to shift. To rise, just a bit, and to take me with it. I tuned into HiC and asked, "What's this about". I didn't get an immediate answer, but I did begin to "come out" of the fear state--the one where wrong conclusions are reached and questionable decisions made. The one where I feel very aware of the feeling and very aware of the hypnotism of it.

HiC said, *"This is one of those mornings; one of those mornings when fear is just in the air. Here, let me help you raise your vibration a bit more. Now, isn't that better?"* Sure enough, the swelling in my belly begin to subside, as if I had taken in a slug of energy and was digesting it. *"Also, you have more work to do on your addiction to fear. You've come a long way, but you've still a ways to go. There's a lot fear swirling around in the world with the various problems and tragedies going on. More than usual, with the full moon and the buildup in momentum for fanaticism. So, let's continue to work on this."*

I got up, fed the cat and the dog, commenced to do yoga and the energy began to loosen a bit more. I went back into a meditative state and got to the point where I finally take in a deep breath of fresh air. I can breathe again. The "spell" is lessening. Light is dawning. My energy continues to increase and bless whatever it is, internally and/or externally, that caused this band of feeling, of vibration, to come and go.

Fuzzy Eyes—See Essence

As Lynne and I were sitting outside this evening I took my glasses off and looked around the yard with "soft eyes". I was more aware of the play of light and dark with each other and not the details. At that point I was transported into 5D Reality. Everything seemed to glow from within. Everything was lit by an inner light and the only difference between the bright and dark areas was the degree of lightness and darkness.

I said to her that it looked like a Renoir painting, with the glow from within being the more obvious appearance than the sharp view of individual items. Lynne said, "I guess he must have needed glasses". We giggled.

This ability to look with "soft" or "fuzzy" eyes is one technique I recommend when observing others in our environment and not judging. Squint slightly and look "softly" at others, mentally, emotionally, and spiritually. Doing so turns the seeing from looking outwards and judging inwardly (the body/mind/ personality's process) to looking from Within with Sacred Eyes and a Higher Consciousness and seeing the essence of what is outside.

Questions to Consider

How do you like these stories? Was anything said that was helpful?

Don't these types of experiences seem within reach for you, too?

What sorts of stories do you have to tell?

CHAPTER 11

My Challenge to You

The **Fear** episode above reminds me of the importance of acknowledging my lower vibration feelings when they come up but not dwelling on them, not trying to ferret out the cause. Instead, I'm reminded to go Within, to do my work there, and allow Within to become the predominant feeling for the moment; to allow Higher Consciousness to energize my system and raise my vibration, thereby buzzing off the yuckiness. This takes some discipline, but similar results in the past have shown me the value in doing this--the value of not letting my thoughtforms or feeling forms run away with me in a direction that is counterproductive to my desire for heightened consciousness.

Access to our Higher Consciousness (HiC if you are comfortable with the idea of a personal soul guide), to repeat, is available most directly through meditation--specifically Higher Consciousness Meditation, which is intended to generate the experience of Higher Consciousness or Higher Awareness. HCM will generate the Higher Vibrations that make direct access possible and attract elevated experiences while melting away lower level vibrations and karma. Simple, huh? But challenging to accomplish until we move in that direction firmly and irretrievably.

This Path begins to get easier and easier once begun, and momentum will develop in the direction we want to go and away from the direction we do not want. Seeds planted have to be watered and nurtured. Then they come up. Your personal Garden has to be weeded with the vigilance of staying aware of lower vibration thoughts and feelings.

Notice that I did not say "bad" thoughts and feelings. Dwelling on lower level thoughtforms is merely ignorance. Ignorance of Spirit's power and ignorance of the Law of Cause and Effect. If we knew we wouldn't focus on our pain and suffering, except to recognize them for what they are, worthy of being converted into joy and love.

So, now you know. What are you going to do about it?

Hint: Get to know your HiC. Ask your HiC "What do you want for me?" Then get very quiet, for as long as you need to. The answer may confirm or surprise, assuming you have been doing this sufficiently to develop a relationship with your HiC that permits conversations or other signals. If not, start today to develop that relationship. Learn first to be very quiet. Allow your Higher Consciousness to begin to enter into, to arise into, your awareness. To flood in, ideally, as you get comfortable with this work.

Your awareness of Higher Consciousness might be just a hint of a feeling, at first, a sense of Presence or elevated vibration. Keep at it. It will get stronger and stronger every time you turn

Within. It will get stronger each time you take a Sacred Breath. The more you do it the stronger the Presence becomes. The nature of that relationship will be between the two of you. No rules, just a flowering forth of your 5D Consciousness aided by Him.

A sense Eternity or The ALL, conversations with your HiC, and events as they unfold are among the confirming experiences you may have as you explore. Whatever the type of response you get it will be accompanied by a tangible upsurge in your vibration, in good feelings, happiness, joy, a sense of "yes". The picture may come all at once or gradually. Again--no rules. I hate to be nonspecific, but your relationship with your Soul is unique in the entire Universe. Your adventure together will be like no other, except that it is certain to be Creative and Expansive.

Questions to Consider

What do you think? Will you accept the challenge?

Are you willing to allow for the possibility of Soul contact? Perhaps even a relationship with your own Higher Consciousness?

CHAPTER 12

Conclusion

I know I have offered lots of ideas, techniques, and tips. These are meant to be aids. Not to be systematized or, worse, turned into beliefs. This book is about Being, not becoming, although most of us have to pass through becoming to get to Being. This Being is about being who you already are. An Eternal Being.

Use these writings to learn to relax into your natural state of Higher Consciousness. Don't effort at it, relax into it. That I have offered you an alternative to the Wheel of Birth and Death, of only a 3d existence on Planet Earth. may spark your own, personal exploration of what seems like a new existence. And is. Until you begin to realize that this is what has been waiting in the background all along for you to see it. With your Sacred Eyes.

And so, the remembering begins. Of your Eternal Existence. An ever-expanding experience into your true Self. Remembering to remember. Remembering what you have known all along, in your deepest memory, that you are an Eternity Consciousness in a limited physical body, on a glorious, limited planet in the outback of the Milky Way Galaxy. Take delight in the ride.

Jesus and others lived lives of Eternal Beings, as well-- experienced and lived lives in their Higher Consciousness most of the time. These lives were examples of how it can be for you, too, if you follow their example into your own Higher Consciousness. In addition, Jesus, and others (Babiji and Sri Yukteswar Giri from the Hindu tradition, for example) have returned from the Other Side in recognizable form to say "See, I am an Eternal Being. And so are you. There is Life on the Other Side."

I have known this, on some level, since 1989 when I went to the funeral of my friend Leo and experienced him as being there at the memorial service, filling the building with his Presence. I stashed that experience away as an unusual figment of my imagination at the time although, even then I knew that I had experienced something that felt very real. And at every funeral since then I have the same experience, one way or another, of the Soul of the deceased being present for the service. I was especially aware of my mother and father speaking to me shortly after their departures, and my father literally lit up the woods as I walked to get the mail the day after he took his last breath.

It's not surprising that those of considerably higher consciousness than these have returned to remind us of whom and what we are.

These writings are merely reminders. I 'm no Master Teacher or guru. I am merely a mystic—defined as one who believes, nay knows, that direct contact with God, Spirit, and your Higher Self is possible. I know because I have experienced it. My job is to remind myself over and over of this fact, and to remind you, if you are reading this. If you remembered just once a day that you are an Eternity Being or made contact with your Higher Consciousness, you would make great progress.

Not in how to act, but in how to Be. Act first—some form of remembrance, and then let Being expand within yourself. Acknowledge the expansion and relax. You are unlocking doors that have been shut for many an eon and letting what Is, Be.

This is all I have to say, I suppose. I know I will continue to write about this because it is my passion. I'll repeat myself from time to time. It will help to expand my Higher Consciousness and share with you what I discover.

Let us remember together.

May your Illumination be Blessed.

CHAPTER 13

Next Steps

My best wishes for your growth and evolution in Higher Consciousness. If you found this book helpful and you want to engage in personal growth and expansion of your awareness, take advantage of the resources that **our website**, HiCMeditation.com provides.

Studies have shown that if an adult wants to learn something s/he will do so more thoroughly and quickly if s/he uses a variety of learning techniques, each of which supports the other. Go to the site HiCMeditation.com for lots to see and do: a blog, articles, sample chapters, poems, and a "Healthy Home" product page.

Studies have shown that if an adult wants to learn something s/he will do so more thoroughly and quickly if s/he uses a variety of learning techniques, each of which supports the other. These are offered at HiCMeditation.com to support you in your journey:

- Go to the site to sign up for our e-mail list. We'll send you the weekly blog post/ newsletter and let you know when each new book is available.

- Other books currently available as Kindle ebooks and paperbacks:
  o **The Amazing Benefits of Meditation: Living the Life You've Always Wanted to Live.** Free at our website or $.99 at Amazon. It examines the scientific research about meditation and discusses why meditation works the way it does. Available Now.
  o **Homage to Spirit,** a book of spiritual verse intended to elevate the reader into a state of elevated awareness. Available Now.
  o **Six Second Mindfulness Meditations: Exercises to Transform any Moment,** offers suggestions and tools you can use to grow in consciousness daily. Available Now.
- Available soon:
  o **The Laws of Vibration and Attraction** takes a deep dive in to methods you can use to attract good people, circumstances, and things into your life. Available in December 2020.
  o **Meditations for Health and Healing** will explore meditations and exercises to help you feel better and take control of your health. Available February 2021.
- Our website includes over 100 products we have personally found to be helpful in promoting well-being and encouraging a Healthy Home.
- My Facebook webpage **Higher Consciousness Meditation with Blair Abee** with the **Daily Vibe,** 365 aphorisms that will bring a smile to your face and lift your spirits.

- We will be releasing other products and services over the next year. Stay tuned.

Also, consider the following:

> **If you got value from this book please, please, please go to Kindle Review and review this book. Many people do not know that a review, even a short one, is like gold to an author. Exposure by Kindle Books, Google rankings and additional book sales are strongly driven by insightful reviews. Thank you!**

3-Dimensional and 5-Dimensional Author Biographies

This book is one in a series of books that I am writing based on my study of spiritual matters over the past 40+ years and the application of principals that I have learned to my life.

As I began to write about myself, I realized that I had two stories tell. One was the 3-dimensional version: I was born, I have lived, and I will die someday. The other is a 5-

Dimensional version that chronicles the relative brief period of the life of an Eternal Being in the latter part of the 20th and the early part of the 21st Centuries.

Version One; 3-Dimensional

- Russell "Blair" Abee, Jr. was born in a 3-dimensional reality on Planet Earth in the middle of the 20th Century. I'm a "baby boomer" and write books. That's it. Someday, I'll go to heaven, hell, or oblivion.
- I was born to parents in North Carolina who seemed to love each other and loved me a bunch. I have three younger brothers and one sister.
- We went to the Lutheran Church in my youth and believed in Jesus as the only Son of God. I bought it all.
- I went to school, lots of it. In undergraduate school I became an atheist because I concluded that the Jesus story was a fairy tale.
- Graduated. Moved to San Francisco.
- My BA in Political Science and a quarter bought me a cup of coffee in the world of work. Started a business remodeling old Victorian houses to survive and stay in California.
- Went back to school to get a master's degree.
- Met a girl. Got married, had 2 kids, boys, and now, 3 grandchildren, boys.
- Had friends, and a few people I disliked.
- Had different jobs. Owned some businesses. Went into government service as a business consultant.
- Retired after 20 years.
- Will die sometime in the next 30 years.

- Most of my world and its activities seem random, with some interesting coincidences along the way.
- My world is a world of duality—black/ white, good/bad; love/hate, hopes/fears

Version Two: 5-Dimensional

- I, Blair Abee, was born in a 5-Dimensional Reality on planet Earth, in what may be one of many Intelligent Universes. I reincarnated in the middle of the 20th Century after many lifetimes stretching back to the beginning of this Universe and will never "die". That is, my consciousness will never be lost.
- I have a purpose, an Eternal Purpose, which is to grow and develop into my destiny as a Universal Citizen. I am learning to live a Spirit guided life to fulfill my Purpose.
- I chose my parents after considering our past lives together, the karma that was in play because of our previous associations, and the possibility that I may be able to fulfill my Purpose this lifetime, or significantly move myself along the Path. In the process, I might be able to erase much of the karma that I had accumulated with my two life sponsors. (This realization to a bit of time to accept.)
- My childhood and educational career were much the same as described above.
- I moved to San Francisco, California, and started on my spiritual Path and began to work in earnest on my Purpose.
- I began with a Jungian dream workshop and spent many years exploring the Self-Help arena.

- I started doing yoga 43 years ago and began my exploration of Zen Buddhism.
- Met my wife Lynn at a "Be Here Now" workshop and we had an immediate connection/recognition. During our long, somewhat contentious courtship, we burned off a lot of personal and couple karma. It became clearer and clearer that we were Soul Mates, companions in many lifetimes, and compatible on many levels. We married.
- We have two children, Ivan (my stepson and good friend) and Justin (our son together). They chose us and we chose them—Ivan needed two dads. They are Mighty Companions.
- We have had a variety of friends and relatives with whom we have clearly spent lifetimes and generated karma. Some are members of our Soul Group.
- I was strongly influenced by the Buddhist concept of "right livelihood" in my career choices and have managed to live by this principal of doing good work, with compatible, enjoyable people, for most of my work career.
- In the past couple of years, I have really found myself really "waking up" and becoming deeply involved in meditation. This has resulted in developing my own form, Higher Consciousness Meditation. As a result, I have come to know my Soul, my individual Higher Consciousness, and have come to many of the realizations expressed in this book. Most importantly, I have come to experience the idea that we all have within us a Higher Consciousness, the same one fully expressed by Krishna, Jesus, and Buddha, among others.

- I have come to realize that I exist in a 5-Dimensional Universe of infinite complexity, much of which I know nothing about, consciously.
- I am working on my Purpose and being led mostly by Spirit, represented by my Higher Consciousness, which I affectionately call "HiC".
- I know that my physical body will die, that my Consciousness, in my Spirit Body, will be elevated into the realm of the Other Side, and that I will continue my Eternity Career there, learning and growing. More than likely I will come back to Earth, with learnings I have gleaned in this lifetime, and will continue the pursuit of my Purpose when I return.

Acknowledgements

There are many people I would like to acknowledge-- family, friends, co-workers, teachers and more. I thought I would do this at the end, at least for my first book, and not force you to wade through them at the beginning. You know some of them now from my stories, some not. All enormously powerful Beings.

Family
- To my beloved wife Lynne, my best friend (maybe for all time)
- To my children and their families: Ivan, Timmy and Silas, Justin, Christina, Archer and Griffy, Phillip, John, Jim and Barb, John and Mary Katherine, Kate--Mighty Companions all
- To my Mom and Dad, gone in body but not in spirit, and my family lineages: grandparents, sisters, brothers, cousins, nieces, nephews
- My brothers, sister and others: Brian, Stewart, Joan, Miranda, Greg, Craig, Jenny, Isaac, Hanna, and Rita Marie (best sister ever), Leonard, Joseph, Sara, Terry and Johnny, Bobbie and Jack, Millie and Toby, Miriam

and Oliver, Ken, Terry and Johnny, Al and Ruth. Fran and Frank

- Lynne's family: Julie, DD, Doug and Eleanor, Sharon, Sandy, Tom, Gordon, Drury, Dora
- Tracey and Jordon, Jim, Chad, Hal
- To Sasha Dog, Stinson Dog, Cecil Dog, Annie Cat, Cleo Cat, Jasper Cat, Snooper Cat

Hickory Friends and Red Tornados:

- Ginny, Jean H, Jean S, Tina, Susan, Butch, Eddie, David, Mike M, Mike H, Steve, Brent, Gary L, Gary S, Clinton, Frank, Poochie, Flea, Ensor, Jenny, Gina and Frank, Stevie, Melissa, Sally, Hal Q, Ms. Lackey, Ms. Cilley, Mr. Noble, Mr. Miller, Mr. Guy, Coach Barger, Coach Lyerly, Jim, Hal, Kirby

And at the NC SBTDC, mighty companions all:

- Bion, Dan, Barry, Scott, Robin, Mark, Lisa, Carol, Wendy, Bill, Rand, Mike, Tim, Tony, Ron, Larry, Kevin, Mark, Steve, Hellen, Chris, Jackie, Suzanne, Susan, Victor, Bob, George, Cheryl, Jim M, Owen, Paul, Jim B, Jim D, Andy, David, Seth, Allan, Eileen, Dean Jessica, Dean Quiester, Jan, Kathy

To the folks at the SBDC in San Diego

- Mighty companions: Carlos, Sudershan, Carol, Gustavo, Desiree, Paul, Teresa, Marquise, Jill, Maria, Ruben
- Might foes: Debbie, Chris, Patrice, and Melinda. I forgive you all. It was part of the plan. You forced me to dig deep and to move on to something better.

San Diego friends

- Mike, Maria, and Michael, DJean and Michael, Vinand, Daniel

Contra Costa and Solano County SBDC colleagues

- Oscar, Cindy, Sandy, Tim, Paul, April, Tim, Scott R, Tom, Kristin, Ann, and all of my clients at both centers

Vallejo friends
- Paul, Dianna and Rick, Roland, Vic and Nancy, Paula and Robert, Peter, Don, Kay, Fresh Air Vallejo, Coleen, Johnnie, Joanne, Dale, Kay, Jim, Dan, Fred, John, Fred, Dan, Ashwin, Tony, Joseph, Aaron.

Others
- Murugananda, Robert, Julia, Alecia, Charley, Curt, Bonnie, Sydney, Barbara, Chris, Cindy, Cat, Ann, Ann, Jim, Anastasia, Robert, Doug, Corky, George, Pat, Floyd, Bobbie and Ruth, Les, Barden and Terry, Barb and Jim, Christie, Tommy and Susan, Bill and Vange, Our Boy, Ann, Anastasia, Dean Perry, Howard, Zack, Ann, Jim, Ann B, Sara B, Nan and Tom, Mary, Breen and Devon, Trudie and Fred, Ryan, Adam, Kate, Ann and John, Bob, Adam, Sarah and Stan, Tristan, Zack, Chiropractors Tom and Phil.

Teachers
- Jesus, Buddha, Krishna, Rumi, Satchidananda, Yogananda, Babaji, Lao Tzu, Mohammed, Ghandi, Joel, Krishnamurti, Martin, Nelson, John K, Bobby K, Fifth Patriarch, Seth, Werner, Carl, Albert, Abraham, Godfrey, Pearl, Ram Dass, Nirmalananda, George and Judith, Peter, Deepak, Oprah, Eckhart, Mooji, John Stewart, Steven Colbert, John Oliver, Samantha Bee, Trevor Noah, Bill Maher. Teachers all, each in their own way.
- And, lastly, I acknowledge my Higher Consciousness who has been my guide and mentor in writing this book.

To these, and many others, I offer a heartfelt "Thank You" for being in my life and contributing to who I am today.

And to you, dear readers: To all who have read this material and find it at least slightly interesting. Especially those who have had, or are going through tough times right now, and may be benefitted by my words. May you find peace of mind in this lifetime.

Blessings.

Excerpts from <u>Homage to Spirit</u>

My new book of spiritual poetry will be out around November 1, 2020, a couple of weeks from the time of this writing. I hope you will pick it up when it's available. Here is an excerpt:

Beloved

Oh, my Higher Consciousness.
My love, my joy, my peace.
Loving me. Loving through me. Loving.
I open to You,
And know You are there always.

I feel like a Bride.
You the Beloved.
Without which our Union would not exist.
Expand me. Expand, me.
For just an instant, out on the edge of Infinity.
Eternity.

I only must Breathe.
You await my stirring, my remembering.
Our remembering.
I encircle and take You in.
Only You complete the Whole.
For me.
For The ALL.

Illumination

Every moment of Illumination a State of Grace.
Words flashing. Recognition. Agreement.
Illumination comes and goes.
Sometimes floating in from "nowhere",
Sometimes with intention.

Both States of Grace, the first a wowzer.
The latter comes with my wish.
"Illuminate, Elevate, Higher Consciousness"
For my hood, my town, my Universe.
My leaders, my relatives in the Galaxy.

I'm thankful for either. Rarified air.
Shift in..........what? What is that?
????
Location of consciousness?
State of Mind or Mindlessness?

Hard to say and leave no doubt,
The words, such containers ill.
When grasping for the It of It.
Somedays it crystalizes in script.

Far as my human experience will take me,
And one step more, into Heaven, here, now.
Over into the land of Context,
In which the content that is "I" resides.

Why love it so?
It resonates so good.

Higher vibrationly vibration,
There I go grasping for that which can't be grasped.

Because the grasper is grasping with the hand.
Attached to the Isness that does the grasping.
It really can't be grasped—the everything/nothing
That peers out of my eyeholes.

Want more? Head over to my website at
www.HiCMeditation.com with additional poems, books, and
more. Also, at my Facebook page at **Higher Consciousness
Meditation with Blair Abee**, where you can Follow the **Daily
Vibe**, 365 uplifting messages to put a smile on your face is
offered. And book 3 in this series, Six Second Mindfulness
Meditations is out along with Book 6 a book of poetry called
Homage to Spirit.

HIGHER CONSCIOUSNESS SERIES BOOK 1

THE AMAZING BENEFITS OF MEDITATION

Living the Life You Want to Live

Health Joy Relationship
Creativity
Stress
Aliveness Peace

BLAIR ABEE

The Amazing Benefits of Meditation Book

(This book is free if downloaded from this site, $.99 at Amazon. See below.) Recent scientific findings have confirmed what Master Teachers and mystics have known for centuries—meditation can help individuals in so many ways; meditation has many benefits–physical, mental, emotional, and spiritual.

Do you:

- Have a **stressful** life?

- Feel like you are on a never-ending **treadmill**?

- **Have physical, emotional, mental issues** you would like to address?

- Wonder what **inner peace** about your circumstances would feel like?

Do you want to:

- **Feel** better?

- Learn how to do **personal healing work** to address concerns and challengers you have?

- Improve your sense of **well-being**?

- Feel more in control of your mental, emotional, physical, and spiritual **health**?

GET FREE

SIX SECOND MINDFULNESS MEDITATIONS

*Exercises
to Transform
Any Moment*

BLAIR ABEE

Six Second Mindfulness Meditations book

The short, 6 second mindfulness practices offered herein are designed to put you back into a place of peace and contact with your Soul; to, if only for a moment, remind yourself of who you are, an Eternal Being of Higher Consciousness, making it easier to cope with the world and to grow and evolve into your Self.

Among the benefits of mindfulness meditations are:
- They are one of the best ways to "get into the moment", be become acutely aware of this present moment and the fullness of Now. Right here. Now.
- They can be done silently and quickly. In an instant you can find yourself having been "raised up" or "expanded into" an elevated state of Consciousness.
- A sense of peace descends, and all seems right with the world. Even if you are in 7:00 am stop and go traffic you may find yourself feeling tolerant of that numbskull who just cut you off without looking to see where you were.

John Kabat-Zinn's research at the University of Massachusetts Medical Center has shown that mindfulness exercise can have the following, significant, almost magical benefits:

- Create a greater sense of well-being
- Help relieve stress
- Treat heart disease
- Reduce chronic pain
- Alleviate depression
- Relieve eating disorders
- Treat anxiety

The book is full of tips, triggers, and reminders to help you tap into Spirit

Book Available at Amazon Kindle in E-book and Paperback Form

PURCHASE NOW

HIGHER CONSCIOUSNESS SERIES BOOK 6

HOMAGE TO SPIRIT

Poems to Elevate Consciousness

BLAIR ABEE

Homage to Spirit: Exercises to Elevate Consciousness

Every so often I get an urge to write a poetry. I have never thought of myself as a poet, only a guy inspired to write. And I just have to do it. Often it just comes pouring out. And I enjoy creating it as I read it. The words just flow, and they are almost always about a new realization I have about my spiritual unfolding. And unfolding and unfolding.

I take liberty with the genre in many ways, including not rhyming or rhythming. I never know what's going to unfold, until it already has. Images come, inspiration leaps, ideas flow and onto the page if I'm lucky enough to have paper around.

My recent Kindle books have been on the subject of meditation and related topics: The Amazing Benefits of Meditation and Higher Consciousness Meditation. This book puts into verse many of the same ideas I have about humanity and the human condition:

- That we are Eternal Beings occupying very complicated biomechanical vehicles, but have so come to identify with the vehicle, and its needs, that we have lost sight of who we really are.
- That the stress, unhappiness, and suffering we all experience, mentally, physically, emotionally, and spiritually comes directly from that identification, especially the identification with the on-board computer, the human mind.
- That we can reclaim our true selves through meditation and other techniques designed to interrupt the flow of the mind's running commentary. The fear thoughts and attempts to control the uncontrollable unfolding of the Universe instead of cooperating with Spirit for Universal Good.

These poems capture my ideas is the rhythmic, mystical language of verse.
Book Available at Amazon Kindle in E-book and Paperback Form

PURCHASE NOW

Made in the USA
Coppell, TX
01 June 2021